Essential
PICASSO

First published in 1999 by
DEMPSEY PARR
Queen Street House
4 Queen Street
Bath BA1 1HE

Created and produced for Dempsey Parr by
FOUNDRY DESIGN AND PRODUCTION,
a part of The Foundry Creative Media Co. Ltd,
Crabtree Hall, Crabtree Lane
Fulham, London, SW6 6TY

ISBN: 1-84084-512-0

A copy of the CIP data for this book is available from
the British Library, upon request

The right of Laura Payne to be identified as the author of this
work has been asserted in accordance with Section 77 of the
Copyright, Designs and Patents Act of 1988.

The right of Dr Julia Kelly to be identified as the author
of the introduction to this book has been asserted in
accordance with Section 77 of the Copyright, Designs
and Patents Act of 1988.

Printed and bound in Singapore.

Essential
PICASSO

LAURA PAYNE

Introduction by Dr Julia Kelly

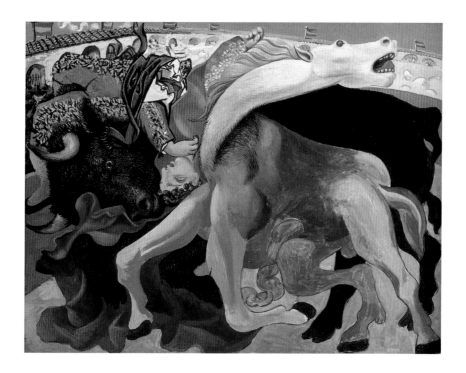

CONTENTS

CONTENTS

INTRODUCTION

WHEN Picasso died at the age of 91 in April 1973, he had become one of the most famous and successful artists of his time. His career had spanned most of the twentieth century and he had taken part in some of the most important art

movements of that century. A creator of a vast number of paintings, sculptures, drawing, etchings, constructions and ceramics, his natural talent and versatility seemed boundless as he passed effortlessly from one medium to another and from one style to the next. His ability to promote himself and his work was without precedent, contributing to a general shift during the twentieth century in the public perception of the artist, from the instinctive creative genius to the careful controller of artistic personae and guises. The art historian Sam Hunter once wrote that 'Picasso, the man and the artist, has cast a spell on his age'. Picasso was, and still is, often seen as a magician by writers and critics, a metaphor that captures both the sense of an artist who is able to transform everything around him at a touch and a man who can also transform himself, elude us, fascinate and mesmerise us and then disappear. Picasso's enduring fascination rests on this Protean element in his character, as his life and work continue to invite countless scholarly interpretations, and exhibitions of his work continue to attract thousands of visitors.

An artist's life is not always seen as integral to his or her work: we feel that great work can stand alone. Picasso's work certainly does to a striking extent, but at the same time he is one of the most autobiographical of artists. He once claimed 'the way I paint is my way of keeping a diary', suggesting a close relationship between art and life. Picasso's life was a long and varied one, encompassing many different locations and homes, several wives and mistresses and their children, as well as important and influential relationships with other artists, poets and writers around him. Indeed, throughout his life Picasso's paintings reflected his surroundings and environments, his changing

domestic circumstances and his perceptions of his own appearance and abilities. As one style succeeded another, a constant theme in Picasso's work was his own life, making him one of the most human and approachable of artists. He was always drawn, in one way or another, to the basic things around him, to what he knew best.

Picasso was born Pablo Diego José Francisco de Paula Juan Nepumuceno María de los Remedios Crispín Crispiniano Santísima Trinidad on the 25th October 1881 in Malaga, in southern Spain. Called Pablo Ruiz Picasso after his father and mother, José Ruiz Blasco and María Picasso López, he later dropped his father's surname to become simply Pablo Picasso. His father was an art school teacher and painter, and Picasso began to draw from an early age. In 1891 the family moved to La Coruña, and a year later Picasso was accepted into the School of Fine and Applied Arts there, where his father had become a professor. As early as 1894, aged 13, he produced his first oil paintings, including portraits of his family, and in 1895 he began to exhibit and sell his work on a small scale. The same year the family moved again, to Barcelona, where Picasso entered the Art School.

Barcelona would be an important centre for Picasso for the next few years. There he would make his first artistic friendships and allegiances, with Manuel Pallarès, Carlos Casagemas and Jaime Sabartés (who would later become Picasso's trusted secretary). By the turn of the century Picasso had begun to associate with the artists and writers of Els Quatre Gats in Barcelona, the 'Four Cats' tavern that provided a meeting place for like-minded Catalan artists who looked towards the avant-garde ferment in Paris. Picasso had been producing large religious paintings, such as *First Communion* or *Science and Charity* (1896), but in his new bohemian circle he began to contribute drawings to Catalan journals, to design posters and flyers, and to make portraits of his new friends and fellow youthful artists, some of which were shown at Els Quatre Gats in his first solo exhibition in 1900.

Paris was the desired destination of these young artists, and in October 1900 Picasso made his first trip there in the company of Casagemas, with whom he rented a studio. Picasso visited the Louvre, and set up a contract with a Catalan dealer, Pere Mañach, to act as his representative in Paris. Casagemas had a disastrous love affair with his model, Germaine and the two painters returned to Barcelona, where they parted company. In early 1901 Picasso discovered that Casagemas had committed suicide in Paris. In May that year, he went back to Paris, moving into the studio of the sculptor Manolo, and in the autumn he created several haunting works in memory of his dead friend.

Picasso only settled in Paris in 1904, having spent a few difficult years with no fixed studio and little artistic success. Whilst back in Barcelona in 1903, he had produced his Blue Period works, which seemed to reflect his experience of relative poverty and instability, depicting beggars, street urchins, the old and frail and the blind. The large canvas *La Vie* expressed the anxiety and indecision of the painter's vocation. In Paris, these subjects and their handling, with their sombre shades and reduced palette, began to make way for the works of the Rose Period: images of groups of travelling acrobats and circus performers. Picasso became friends with the poets Max Jacob, Guillaume Apollinaire and André Salmon, and these friends, the 'bande à Picasso', would meet at the Le Lapin Agile café. He lived and worked in the Bateau-Lavoir in the rue Ravignan in Montmartre, a ramshackle collection of artists' studios, and he became involved with his first artistically significant mistress, Fernande Olivier, who moved into his studio in 1905.

At this time, Picasso was very open to artistic influences around him, and events of these years would have a major effect on him: the exhibition of Fauve works, particularly those of Matisse, in the 1905 Salon d'Automne, as well as large retrospectives of Ingres, Gauguin and Cézanne. Picasso responded to the new avant-garde developments of the Fauve painters in Paris by exploring new directions himself, creating his own ground-breaking style. A visit to Gósol, in the Spanish Pyrenées, seemed to provide the breakthrough, as Picasso's work became less symbolist and more reductive, focusing on the simplified and monumentalised forms of the human figure. A portrait of Gertrude Stein, his new patron, was completed after this visit in 1906, and was a striking example of his new sculptural approach to his art.

As Matisse exhibited his *Blue Nude* and Derain his *Bathers* in 1907, Picasso countered with the work that became one of the cornerstones of his fame, which we now know as *Les Demoiselles d'Avignon*. In this work, he began to incorporate African influences into his work. These, combined with the influence of Cézanne, and Picasso's new friendship with the painter Georges Braque, steered the direction of his work for the next few years. Picasso's work caught the attention of the young and relatively wealthy dealer Daniel-Henry Kahnweiler, who started to buy his art; over the next few years he set up an exclusive contract that would grant Picasso financial security. In 1909, the artist was able to move to a new studio on the Boulevard de Clichy, and in 1912 he moved again, to Montparnasse, a new, exciting artistic centre.

Picasso was spending more and more time with Braque, whose work had been described as 'Cubist' by the critic Louis Vauxcelles in 1908. Between 1910 and 1912, the two artists would work in each other's studios, holiday together and produce work of a very similar appearance. They concentrated on still lifes, café subjects, table tops, musical instruments and portraits, depicted in subdued tones in a faceted style that was quickly proclaimed a revolution in artistic representation and conception. In 1912, they began to introduce pasted papers, false wood-graining and other materials into their works, posing a radical challenge to 'high' art's traditional insistence on beautiful and precious objects.

By the time of his first large retrospective exhibition in Munich in early 1913, Picasso's work had begun to be shown internationally, as well as promoted in the critical writings of Apollinaire and Salmon, and he had begun to achieve some financial success. The outbreak of war was a considerable setback, scattering his friends and supporters far and wide -- Apollinaire and Braque were sent to the front, and Kahnweiler, as a German national, took refuge in Switzerland. During the First World War, which Picasso spent between Paris and Barcelona, he began to frequent a new circle, including the dealer Léonce Rosenberg, the poet Jean Cocteau, the composer Stravinsky and the dancer Diaghilev.

These new contacts brought about several changes in Picasso's life. In 1917 he began work on the ballet *Parade* in collaboration with the Ballets Russes. He visited Italy, particularly Rome, Florence and Pompeii, and met a ballet dancer of Russian origin, Olga Kokhlova, whom he married in 1918. He began to move in higher social circles, and that year acquired an elegant new flat and separate studio in the rue La Boëtie, reflecting this change. Picasso's artistic production at this time was diverse: some of his works were still pursuing the Cubist explorations started a few years earlier; others featured a neo-Classical style that owed much to Ingres. The subjects of this new neo-Classicism included monumental female figures, Mediterranean backdrops and depictions of maternity. In 1921 Picasso and Olga's son Paulo was born.

During the early 1920s in Paris, Dada and Surrealism were the new revolutionary artistic movements, and Picasso, by this time in his forties, did not actively participate in these movements. He was, however, held up by them as an artistic hero, particularly by the Surrealists, whose leader André Breton was an ardent admirer of Picasso and who helped him to sell *Les Demoiselles d'Avignon* in 1924. In 1925, his large work *Three Dancers* showed another stylistic departure, this time incorporating some of the mood of Surrealist art works, which explored the power of the liberated unconscious mind.

Picasso's work of this period was marked by an increasing deformation of the human figure, sometimes of an almost violent nature. Picasso would later describe his own painting as a 'sum of destructions'. In 1926 he produced a large work based on the form of a guitar. This consisted of a torn piece of cloth from which nails emerged, pointing towards the viewer. Towards the end of the 1920s, he began to produce drawings of his wife Olga as a screaming and sharp-toothed monster. In 1927, as his marriage became increasingly antagonistic, Picasso began an affair with Marie-Thérèse Walter, then a seventeen-year-old schoolgirl, and her features had begun to pervade his art, in works showing rounded and sensual female forms.

Picasso also began to produce sculpture again in the late 1920s, a medium which he had not explored since his Cubist sculptures and constructions. He learned to weld metal in the studio of Julio González, and there he created large metal-rod constructions, as well as producing many drawings for sculpture. In 1931 he began to work in a large sculpture studio in a converted stables in his chateau at Boisgeloup, outside Paris, which he had acquired the previous year. He worked on a series of large portrait busts of Marie-Thérèse, whose swollen and bulbous forms reflected that of many of Picasso's paintings of her of the early 1930s. Here, and during summer holidays spent at Juan-les-Pins, he also started to include real objects in his sculptural assemblages, often grafting together objects and then casting them to produce strange hybrids, a technique which would be a marked feature of his sculptural production in years to come.

Picasso had now acquired real status in the art world, as an important series of exhibitions of his work in Paris, London and New York in the early 1930s demonstrated. In 1932, Christian Zervos, the editor of the important Parisian art periodical *Cahiers d'Art*, issued the first volume of a *catalogue raisonné* of Picasso's work, which aimed to provide as complete a record as possible of his output. In response to this, and his increased fame, Picasso began to date the vast number of drawings and paintings that he was producing with a much greater precision than before. He was creating large series of etchings, such as those for Balzac's *Unknown Masterpiece* in the 1920s, and during the 1930s he produced around 100 etchings that were gathered together for the dealer and publisher Ambroise Vollard.

In his earlier work, Picasso had been drawn to the figure of the

Harlequin as a sort of alter ego, and as a physical means of exploring the superimposition of coloured planes through the character's costume. In the 1930s, however, the Minotaur held sway. Picasso had depicted bullfighting scenes since his earliest drawings, and returned again and again to this most Spanish of themes. In the Minotaur, he had the opportunity of reinventing the Spanish bull to create a complex figure, more in line with his explorations of the darker side of human nature. The Minotaur stood for illicit passion as well as grotesque physical forms and, in its incarnation as a blinded beast requiring a guiding hand, for human frailty and vulnerability.

Picasso visited Spain in 1933 and 1934: these were to be his last visits to his native country. In 1936 civil war broke out in Spain, and Picasso became an supporter of the Republicans, who named him director of the Prado museum in Madrid as a symbolic gesture. He had befriended Paul Eluard, the Surrealist poet and committed Communist, and came to know other figures in his circle such as Roland Penrose, Man Ray, and his fellow photographer Dora Maar, who became Picasso's lover. His domestic arrangements were complicated. Although separated from Olga, he was not divorced, and he was obliged to house Marie-Thérèse, who had given birth to their daughter, Maya, in 1935.

Dora Maar found him a studio in Paris in the rue des Grands Augustins, where he would paint *Guernica (1907)* and she, knowing its significance, would photograph its making for posterity.

Guernica was the most explicitly political work that Picasso had produced to date. He had moved in anarchist circles in Barcelona at the turn of the century and had always taken an interest in wider political events, but never before had he commented on them in such a striking and powerful way. *Guernica* was immediately recognised as a work of great importance, a monumental statement about the general inhumanity of war, and the painting toured England in 1938. Other paintings of 1937, such as a series of *Weeping Women*, suggested a similar humanist response to the events of the Spanish Civil War, but were also based on personal circumstances, being portraits of Dora Maar with her characteristic and extravagant clothes and hats.

Picasso's paintings of the Second World War continued to express the violence and oppression of the times, but in a much more subtle and muted way. Picasso turned to the humble objects around him, to still lifes of food (a scarce resource), or of symbolic skulls and candles, or alternatively to portraits of Olga with her features and limbs twisted and contorted into uncomfortable grimaces and poses. His limited and introspective subject matter was in part a political response to the stifling restrictions of the Vichy regime, but it also reflected the privations and constraints of his war-time situation, as he remained in Paris, keeping a low profile, while many of his friends fled.

The fact that Picasso had remained in Paris during the Occupation meant that he was heralded as a symbol of Liberation as the war came to an end. In 1944 he joined the French Communist Party and a retrospective selection of his work was shown in the October Salon de la Libération. His *Dove* lithograph (1949) was used as the poster for the World Peace Congress. Into the next decade he produced several large-scale works with political themes, such as the *Charnel House* (1945), *Massacre in Korea* (1951) and the *War and Peace* murals (1952) – unfortunately none of these pictures were available for reproduction in this book. Picasso also became an international figurehead for the Communist movement, including producing a now-famous portrait of Stalin in 1953. At the same time Picasso began to strengthen his links with the south of France, where he would eventually settle. In 1946 he painted the chateau at Grimaldi in Antibes with Mediterranean and mythological themes, and a year later he began to produce ceramics in the Madoura pottery in Vallauris.

Picasso had a public face, marked by political allegiance, but he was also, in much of his artistic production, pursuing an intensely private path. During the war he met Françoise Gilot, who gave him two children: Claude, in 1947, and Paloma, in 1949. Their relationship was intense and at times stormy, as Françoise, a painter in her own right, was keen to make her artistic mark. By 1951, Picasso was also involved with Geneviève Laporte, and divided his time between several locations including Paris, Saint-Tropez, and Vallauris, where he had rented a villa, La Galloise. In 1953, Françoise left La Galloise and Picasso, taking their children. That winter he created an extensive series of 180 drawings known as the *Verve suite*, depicting circus performers, clowns, Cupid figures, and elderly painters studying young female models, suggesting a period of soul-searching. The painter and model motif in particular in this series, as a way of exploring the artist's own persona and function, would become a dominant theme in what we now see as Picasso's 'late' work.

By 1955, Picasso had settled in the south of France, and would return to Paris only once more before his death. Living and working in a series of villas and chateaux, he was producing as diverse a range of work as ever, including wooden sculptures and a mural for the UNESCO building in Paris, but a sense of his own artistic identity was paramount. Large sequences of paintings after Delacroix' *Femmes d'Alger,* Velasquez' *Las Meninas* and Manet's *Déjeuner sur l'Herbe* indicated an awareness of the stature and success he had achieved, as he measured

himself up against the Old Masters. Rather than look outwards, Picasso was drawn to his own immediate surroundings: his studio interiors at La Californie in Cannes, and at Notre-Dame-de-Vie in Mougins, his last studio, and portraits of his wife Jacqueline Roque, whom he met in the late 1940s and married in 1961. He was also inspired to look back over his own life, in the etchings known as the *Suite 347* (1968), many of which dealt with the process of ageing.

Picasso's last works reflected one of the dualities that his work throughout his career had expressed: a kind of Spanish *terribilità*, an exploration of dark forces, violence and terror, combined with an exuberant vitality, encompassing all created things. Some of his final self-portraits stare out at the viewer with an anguished fear of death: frail, skull-like and desperate. Yet we cannot forget the extraordinary flowering of sexuality in Picasso's late works, the passionate and acrobatic couplings, and the liberated handling of paint in loose and flamboyant brushstrokes. If he faced mortality with apprehension and poignant regret, that was only because he had experienced his life so intensely.

DR JULIA KELLY

BULLFIGHT (1901)
Courtesy of Christie's Images

T HE intensity of colour and vibrant rhythm of the brushstrokes introduces Picasso's favourite, recurrent theme – the bullfight. His artistic dynamism is hurled into the passion of his subject matter. One can sense the excitement, the violence and ultimate challenge of life or death glowing from the canvas. These are issues that haunt Picasso's work, surfacing thematically over the years: notions of sex, death, rebirth and the paradoxes they create. It is a bizarre contradiction of glory and repugnance, beauty and deformity, spiritual versus earthly physicality.

Conscious of the Minotaur myth and its association with his Spanish roots, Picasso swirls his brush across the canvas like the matador twirling his red cape, connoting blood and passion. Using a trick developed here, and repeated in later works, the perspective means that the viewer is part of the audience, gazing down, as the scene fans out in a series of brightly colour banded ellipses. The brilliant handling of colour and light equates dark with the death of the lanced bull and light with the life and passion of the sun-topped arena, burning in intense shimmering golden yellow paint. The bright gold is repeated in the matador's costume, allying him symbolically at the moment of death with the implied sun motif of life.

IN THE CAFÉ (C. 1901)

Courtesy of Christie's Images

*C*AFÉ life, either in Paris or Barcelona, was another regular theme for the 19-year-old Picasso, who was experimenting with new styles, characterisations and handling of various mediums. This work is probably part of a series of watercolours and India ink sketches on paper, completed in Paris in 1901, in which he studied the 'society' prostitute and was undoubtedly influenced by Degas's and Toulouse-Lautrec's similar treatment of this subject.

Here we see a flamboyantly dressed woman, sitting alone, symbolically separated from the group of well-to-do men in their top hats. Her solitary presence implies status as a prostitute, as a women of rank would never have been unaccompanied. The flamboyance is implied by subtle use of colour on the hat, face and dress in a painting of otherwise subdued tones.

Picasso had returned to Paris from Spain in May 1901 to prepare for his first exhibition at Ambroise Vollard's – the young, pushy gallery owner who became a lifelong friend and dealer of Picasso's work. (In his middle years, Picasso explored new themes and artistic imagery in a series of etchings which became known as the *Vollard Suite*.) This café scene was probably one of several pieces desperately painted in a last-minute bid to fill exhibition space.

DETAIL OF CHILD WITH A DOVE
(BOY WITH A DOVE) (1901)
National Gallery, London. Courtesy of Topham

THIS famous oil painting represents a radical change of direction from Picasso's early, more Impressionist works. The bold black outlining – a direct influence of Gauguin and Van Gogh whom Picasso saw at Vollard's gallery – rich colour and depth of energy are certainly neo-Impressionist and anticipate Fauvism, a later post-Impressionist movement whose name means 'wild animal'.

The child subject matter is an interesting departure from the many café scenes and entertainer portraits and was Picasso's attempt to explore more intensely personal issues. The dove makes its debut as a significant recurrent motif throughout his career, even appearing in Cubist works, such as *Still Life of a Pigeon* (1920), which is tonally very similar to this work. It relates to childhood and his father, (an impoverished art teacher who became obsessed with drawing the pigeon life cycle). Picasso soon loathed his father's artistic dominance over his prodigious talent and while a student is recorded as saying that 'In art one must kill one's father'. This oedipal mandate is interpreted as the corner stone of the Picasso creative process and commentators are overly fond of discovering some patricidal twist in his work.

Although apparently simplistic in style, this work's reductionist handling of space and colour is highly sophisticated for this period, underlying its importance in Picasso's development.

Still Life of a Pigeon (1919)
Courtesy of Christie's Images. (See p. 94)

SABARTÉS (LE BOCK OR GLASS OF BEER) (1901)

Pushkin Museum, Moscow. Courtesy of Art Resource

*A*S IN THE following picture, *The Two Saltimbanques* (1901), Picasso returns to a café or bar setting in order to study his handling of colour and spatial dimensions in oil. Here we start to witness a deliberate distortion of form with Sabartés's Mannerist long tapering fingers and the exaggerated shape of the glass. The painting cleverly conjures up sentiments of languor and tedium, enhanced by the overall blue tone, which also started to infiltrate the slightly earlier *Child with a Dove* (also 1901).

Sabartés represents the onset of Picasso's intense Blue Period – a colouring much favoured by the French Symbolist movement, currently sweeping the art world at the turn of the century. Yet the tonal qualities also reflect Picasso's own sombre, disturbed mood after the shocking suicide of his close friend, fellow artist Casagemas. Picasso's creative reaction to guilt about his friend's death begins to surface in this early, melancholy, Blue Period work.

Here Picasso features another loyal Spanish friend, Jaime Sabartés, who on joining Picasso in Paris started a life-long association with him, becoming his biographer, legend-monger and secretary. Much of what is known about his early life is often credited to Sabartés's accounts.

The Two Saltimbanques (1901)
Pushkin Museum, Moscow.
Courtesy of Giraudon. (See p. 24)

THE TWO SALTIMBANQUES (1901)

Pushkin Museum, Moscow. Courtesy of Giraudon

Paulo Picasso (1924)
The Picasso Museum, Paris. Courtesy of Giraudon.
(See p. 114)

*T*his is regarded as Picasso's exploration of another enduring image from his private artistic rhetoric – the circus. In this highly expressive and distinctive work, Picasso experiments carefully and playfully with the colour. The blue tone seeps through, but is allowed to deliberately counterbalance and clash with the garishness of the vivid orange. This neo-Impressionist technique of clashing colour symbolises the paradoxical joy of entertainment and the sadness of the clown's tears. Its striking use conveys a sense of fun, although this is powerfully checked and held in place by an aura of melancholy.

Picasso often depicted himself as Harlequin – the facile entertainer, artistic rogue and jester from the traditional medieval touring repertoire of the Italian Commedia dell'Arte. In this case, the harlequin figure does not seem to be a projection of the artist, but the circus subject matter gains pace in the subsequent Picasso Rose Period, with many of his contemporaries transformed pictorially into key troupe figures.

An interesting return is made to the harlequin theme with the 1924 portrait of his young son, *Paulo Picasso*, now dressed as harlequin like his father. It is an elaboration on the theme of young pretender as a biological and artistic projection of himself.

MOTHER AND CHILD (MATERNITY) (1901)

Courtesy of Topham

*T*HE religious connotations of any picture involving a mother and child are inevitable and this iconic statement is one of a series of 'Madonnas' painted during the Blue Period. Picasso repeatedly combines the themes of religion and poverty as his development of the female figure moves away from the sexual allusions encompassed in prostitute images, to the more hallowed portrayal of the mother figure.

The almost monochromatic use of blue in this period, and its traditional association with the Madonna, are superbly combined to produce a set of haunting, almost ghostly images. Notably, many of the Blue Period women are bowed as if carrying a heavy emotional burden.

Here the handling of space has a distinctive feel. The spatial structure is clearly defined and organised in horizontal bands crossed by the vertical lines of the upright chair. This grid-work of lines is beautifully disturbed by the gentle motion of the mother's lovingly bent head kissing the child. The flowing line is echoed in the cascading folds of the mother's wrap, redeveloped in a similar figure in *La Vie* (1903).

The highly expressive style is reminiscent of the 16th-century Spanish Mannerist master, El Greco (1541–1614), whom Picasso studied during his brief time in Madrid in 1896, reflected in the exaggerated, enlarged hands and the long, tapering fingers.

La Vie (1903)
Cleveland Museum of Art. Courtesy of Giraudon. (See p. 36)

MOTHER AND CHILD (MATERNITY) (1901)

Courtesy of Christie's Images

*T*HIS painting is often wrongly dated to 1903–04 but is actually contemporary with the previous picture. Apart from the shared subject matter, this picture has a looser, lighter and less iconic feel. Interestingly, the medium is oil painted on wood, reminiscent of the early Byzantine technique for painting religious icons.

The work also has a strong Gauguin-like quality, with the depth and richness of colour set in distinct simplistic blocks and the emphasis on a decorative line. This can be seen in the strange, exaggerated Mannerist hands of the mother and the lyrical shape of her body which almost makes her flow out of the countryside around her with the strong swirling brushwork of her skirt and underlying ground. She is a disturbing combination of holy woman and pagan earth mother as she embraces the odd, oversized foetal-shaped child, whose strange shape and size brings to mind the disproportionate early depictions of the Holy Child.

The rural backdrop is also a typical setting for early Renaissance Madonnas, but, in this Modernist piece, Picasso uses this pastoral scene to challenge classical, representational and aesthetic concepts concerning the portrayal of the Madonna.

Mother and Child (1901)
Courtesy of Topham. (See p. 26)

SELF-PORTRAIT (1901)

The Picasso Museum, Paris. Courtesy of Giraudon

*P*ICASSO painted this self-portrait in Paris in late 1901 before he left for Barcelona in January 1902. This is a period of personal confusion for Picasso, well represented in this oil painting. In another sombre, unnerving work of the Blue Period, the heavy black coat, hair and beard, combined with Picasso's intensity of gaze, create a heightened sense of the macabre. It is almost a death mask with the framed whiteness of the face and hollowed-out cheeks.

This is a young man who seems old beyond his years. He is, without doubt, parodying one of Van Gogh's self-portraits with this air of austerity, as well as an El Greco-style monk or ascetic. However, Picasso, like his favourite Old Masters, was also in a formative period of destitution, struggling with his potential talent while living off food parcels from friends.

When this portrait is compared with the later jovial and more juvenile face of 1907, one can clearly see the affectation of age. The later portrait begins the collapse of recognised form as part of the build up to Cubism. But here we are confronted with a sense of cold alienation, a confused artist torn between excitement at being in Paris and homesickness for Spain.

Self-Portrait (1907)
Prague National Gallery. Courtesy of Giraudon. (See p. 62)

ANGEL FERNANDEZ DEL SOTO (1903)

Courtesy of Christie's Images

IN 1903 Picasso, shattered by the suicide of his close friend Casagemas, reflects this mood of melancholia in this sombre portrait of acquaintance and aspiring fellow artist, Angel Fernandez del Soto. Picasso returned to the Barcelona studio he once shared with Casegemas and started to paint again with Del Soto. He was possibly trying to recapture his former life and dead friend, as this work can be read ironically as a death mask with downcast eyes and a disturbing stillness. The inclusion of blue is a footnote to Picasso's Blue Period, now in full flow. However, the sketch heralds the later Rose Period of *Saltimbanques* (1905) and the similar transitional portrait *Woman in a Chemise* (1904-05), in which a warmer palette starts to infuse. The delicacy of line and tone also captures an essence of inner beauty more associated with the Rose Period, but missing from Picasso's portraiture of this time.

In fact, Picasso's later 1903 images of Del Soto depict him in a more traditional habitat – the bar. Picasso's friends enjoyed welcoming him back to the Barcelona café scene as they caroused around the brothels together. Picasso ultimately tires of Del Soto's drunken laziness, moving out of the memory-filled studio. This productive period saw more than 50 works completed in just 14 months.

Woman in a Chemise (1904–05)
Courtesy of the Tate Gallery, London. (See p. 42)

LA CELESTINE (CARLOTTA VALDIVIA) (1903)

Musée Picasso, Paris. Courtesy of Giraudon/Art Resource

*T*HIS highly concentrated composition is one of many damaged, forlorn characters or street martyrs of Picasso's intense Blue Period. For instance, Carlotta is the one-eyed procuress from a Fernando de Rojas (*c.* 1475–*c.* 1538) play. Almost total renunciation of colour exaggerates the sense of despair in this repugnant image from the depth of the Blue Period. Picasso is quoted as saying that blue reflected his sadness after Casagemas's death but this mood no doubt included guilt. The two men had parted on bad terms and, after the suicide, Picasso briefly took up with Casagemas's married lover, Germaine, whose refusal to marry Casagemas had prompted his death. It was an emotional tangle.

Picasso seems to paint himself in to an artistic corner, and the impasse of style and restriction of palette is particularly evident. Only the intense, emotive face and expressive folds of the clothes, as seen in the similarly hooded figure of *Mother and Child (Maternity)* (1901), manage to create a sense of movement in the otherwise highly restrained work, though this lack of movement deliberately accentuates the figure's gaunt frailty.

The allegory of blindness intimated here regularly pursued Picasso throughout his life like a shadow and he once said that painters' eyes should be put out 'like bullfinches to make them sing better'.

Mother and Child (Maternity) (1901)
Courtesy of Topham. (See p. 26)

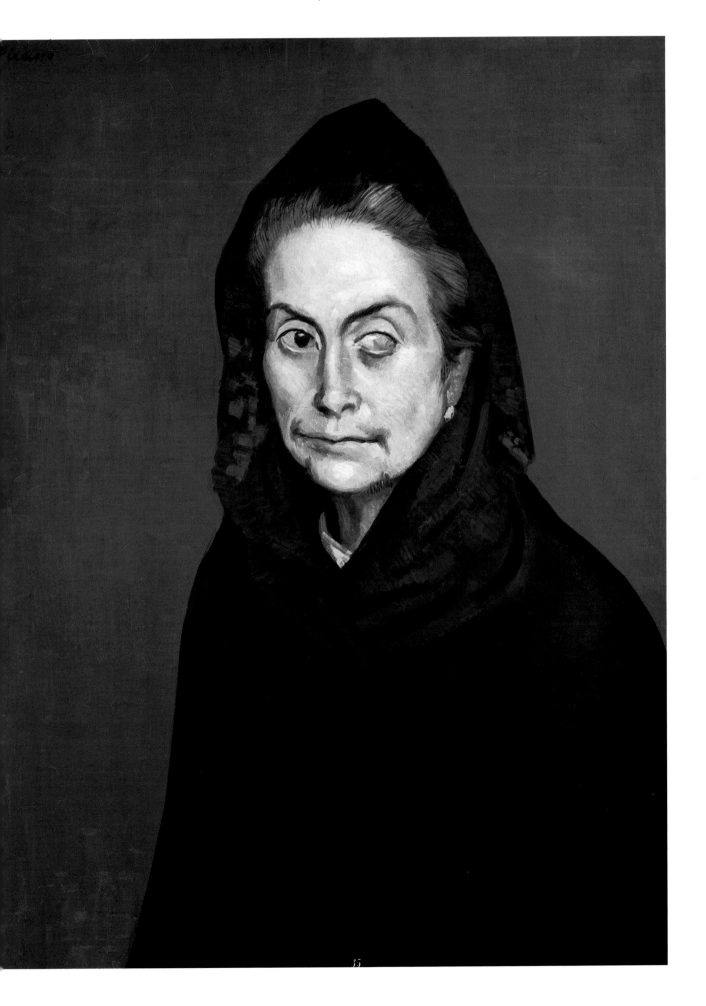

LA VIE (1903)

Cleveland Museum of Art. Courtesy of Giraudon

ALTHOUGH entitled 'Life', this large allegorical picture is about death as Picasso struggled to paint a fitting tribute to his dead friend Casagemas.

In 1903 Picasso returned from Paris to the Barcelona studio he had once shared with Casagemas. He was in a highly emotional state and preliminary *La Vie* studies depict Picasso as a central figure. Set in an artist's studio, Casagemas's final presence is now implied as unfinished canvasses symbolically separate the frail lovers and mother. The figures have little substance in comparison with the solidity of the head and shoulders in *Portrait of Benedetta Canals* (1905).

The blue-green wash establishes the tone of grief and psychological depression and is influenced by the then popular Parisian Symbolists' cycle of life paintings, charting the biblical seven cycles of man. Picasso, like his friend the symbolist poet Apollinaire, was an occult student and the three figures are said to be taken from the Tarot

pack's The Lovers card, depicting Adam's choice between the angel and Eve – namely the age-old conundrum of choice between sacred and profane love. Ironically Picasso worked *La Vie* over his *Last Rites* (c. 1900), symbolically painting 'Life' upon death, which was one of his favourite paradoxical themes.

Portrait of Benedetta Canals (1905)
Picasso Museum, Barcelona. Courtesy of Giraudon. (See p. 46)

THE SOLER FAMILY PICNIC (1903)

Liege Museum. Courtesy of Topham

PAINTED in Barcelona, this work has an over-stylised, superficial finish, and is significantly different from other works completed that year. Its composition is undoubtedly based on Manet's celebrated *Le Déjeuner sur l'Herbe* (1863), which Picasso had admired in the Luxembourg on his first visit to Paris. He returned once more to this theme in his final years.

In this picture, Picasso became dissatisfied with the prosaic subject matter. The depiction of bourgeois life might have been a radical change from the characteristic retinue of waifs and strays of the period, but the shooting picnic is believed to be unfinished.

Benet Soler Vidal, a wealthy tailor, fancied himself as a patron of the arts, and Picasso, despite impoverished means, often appeared as the man about town, dressed in dashing, fashionable waistcoats by exchanging paintings for clothes. For Picasso, dress was an extension of his personality and a symbol of artistic magic. His clothes were never thrown away and many from this time were discovered on his death 70 years later.

This painting originally had a plain background but Soler preferred a traditional landscape, so Picasso later authorised another artist to paint in the trees. As shown here, Picasso restored the blue surround before the painting was re-sold in 1913.

PORTRAIT OF SUZANNE BLOCH
(OPERA SINGER) (1904)

Courtesy of Christie's Images

*T*HIS fascinating transitional picture marks attempts by the artist to pull himself out of the tortuous artistic depths of his intense Blue Period. Colour changes start to appear in sketches, as here, with this cartoonesque drawing of Bloch in Indian ink and sepia wash, and reach fruition at the start of 1905, as the Rose Period, intimated here, begins to supervene. Suzanne Bloch was one of the diverse Bohemian artistic crowd that hung around Montmatre during Picasso's Bateau Lavoir studio period. Sister of the famous violinist,

Seated Woman with a Hat (1971)
Courtesy of Christie's Images. (See p. 254)

Henri Bloch, Suzanne, also immensely musically gifted, later became a famous Wagnerian opera singer.

The heavy, washed lines and satirical, angular face do not really enhance the soft, gentle charms of this talented young woman. However, these heavy caricature techniques evolved throughout Picasso's career into his distinctive portrait style, employed to the end of his career, as in *Seated Woman with a Hat* (1971).

It is not known whether this sketch was carried out for fun, but it does not relate to other female studies during this period. It was possibly a working drawing for a more serious memorable oil study of Bloch, also in 1904, not shown here, which returns to this era's characteristic blue tone and captures the singer's softer, more sensitive features.

WOMAN IN A CHEMISE (1904–05)

Courtesy of the Tate Gallery, London

THIS marks the end of Picasso's Blue Period. The light blue loses its icy frigidity as female beauty and lust return as suitable subject matter. This underscores the absence of real sexual passion in previous works, whose emotional tones are achieved instead by the social comment implicit in the characters' destitute state.

This face is probably of new mistress, Madeleine, featured in a series of erotic drawings, as here, with the light deliberately accented on the exposed breast. The new, shimmering blue-green provides a striking contrast with the ghostly transparency of the chemise, whose folds create notional movement. 'Chemise' may translate as 'night-shirt', underscoring the woman's sexual availability.

In the summer of 1904, Madeleine became pregnant by Picasso, but he pressurised her into having an abortion. In 1968, when this painting resurfaced, he joked, 'Can you imagine me having a son 64 years old?' However, despite starting an affair with another model, Fernande Olivier, Madeleine mother-and-child images appear at the same time as their child would have been born.

Portrait of Benedetta Canals (1905)
Picasso Museum, Barcelona. Courtesy of Giraudon.
(See p. 46)

The dating of the picture is confused. The rigid colouring may place it in late 1904, as his palette did not warm up until early 1905, then incorporating russet hues as in *Portrait of Benedetta Canals* (1905).

LA BELLE FERNANDE (1906)
Courtesy of Christie's Images

ERNANDE is said to have been the first great love of Picasso's life and her impact on this early period is well documented. She was living with a sculptor when she first met Picasso and was said to be lazy and promiscuous. Yet, although she came from the same bohemian Parisian crowd as the painters' models, Fernande exuded more sophistication and refinement. She did not move in with Picasso until 1905 and most of what is known about Fernande comes from her explosive memoirs, which were published, much to Picasso's outrage, in the 1930s.

Early watercolours depict her asleep whilst Picasso watches on, a theme on lust to which the artist returns later in his career with Surrealist-inspired works such as *Rest* (1932). Here, the dream-like quality is ethereal and hallucinatory. It is interesting that Fernande later claimed that they dabbled in opium-smoking as part of their sex life.

Her heavily pronounced head and profile conjures up notions of Greek Classicism, but the heavy-eyed sensualism is dreamily accentuated. Drugs became a way of life and their influence in Picasso's art during this period should be seriously considered. It was the violent suicide of another artist friend, in 1908, that shocked the artist – who found the body – into finally quitting the habit.

Asleep (1932)
Courtesy of Christie's Images.
(See p. 129)

PORTRAIT OF BENEDETTA CANALS (1905)

Picasso Museum, Barcelona. Courtesy of Giraudon

*D*EPICTED here is the beautiful wife of Spanish painter Ricardo Canals, who was a close friend of Picasso's from their formative days together in the artists' watering hole, El Quatre Gats (Four Cats) café in Barcelona. Canals also moved to Montmartre, Paris, where he is said to have taught Picasso etching.

The management of space means that the expansive colouring of the background dwarfs the figure, despite its heightened stature emphasised by the traditional Spanish mantilla head-dress. However, this conflict intensifies the figure's beauty, as the pale face and décolleté are framed by the contrasting black heaviness of the exotic lace. Her downward gaze at the viewer suggests an extra haughty grandeur, contrary to Picasso's portrayal of French women of the same period, a technique he returns to with a portrait of his wife Olga. The fact that Benedetta was from Rome, and was said to have modelled for Renoir and Degas, perhaps explains her notion of superiority, perfectly caught by Picasso.

Although Picasso had returned to his Spanish roots in this painting, the artistic pun probably bears reference to her multi-nationality – that she was an Italian in France and married to a Spaniard. Picasso, too, was a foreigner established in Paris and would settle here for the rest of his life – although he would remain always a Spaniard at heart.

**Portrait of Olga
in an Armchair (1917)**
*The Picasso Museum, Paris.
Courtesy of Giraudon. (See p. 88)*

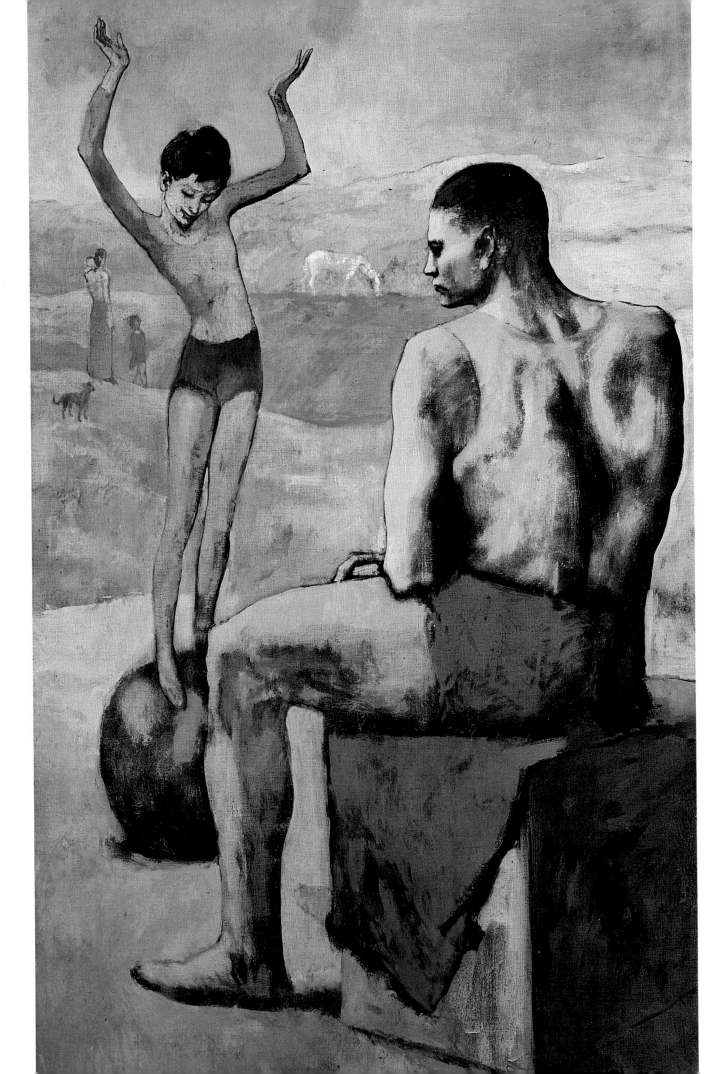

YOUNG ACROBAT ON A BALL (1905)

Pushkin Museum, Moscow. Courtesy of Giraudon

THE year 1905 saw the final collapse of the blue pallet in Picasso's work, as greys and then warm reds were gradually allowed to seep back into the range during the year. His repertoire of thin, gaunt female figures is joined by a troupe of other circus personalities. Fun and optimism, instead of melancholia and social alienation, return as subject matter, though depictions of entertainment are still moderated by the inherent social out-casting of the circus community.

In this painting, the pinky tones of the Rose Period are apparent, though the chilling grey of the acrobat's bodysuit strangely arrests the young girl's fluid animation. Her lithe, rounded motions, echoing the shape of the ball, are in obvious opposition with the square muscular form of the man, whose shape is interrelated with the solid, cubed seat. Like the *Mother and Child (Maternity)* (1901), the strong, upward, angular lines are crossed by a series of horizontal blocks, but in this instance they are allowed to undulate to create a further flowing movement that compliments the rolling force of the girl standing on the ball. The whole picture is a study of stasis versus movement, reflecting an interesting evolution in Picasso's own aesthetic advancement as he moves into this new period.

Mother and Child (Maternity) (1901)
Courtesy of Topham. (See p. 26)

SALTIMBANQUES
(THE FAMILY OF SALTIMBANQUES) (1905)

Chester Dale Collection. Courtesy of the National Gallery of Art,
Washington D.C./Bob Grove

*T*HIS picture is usually seen as the dominant composition of Picasso's Rose Period – the conclusion of developing style, colouring and themes to date. A massive canvas, in fact the largest that Picasso ever worked on at 212.8 x 229.6 cm, (7 x 8 ft), it was the outcome of several preliminary studies, including elements taken from *Young Acrobat on a Ball* (1905). The background was originally a racecourse until Picasso created this barren landscape, which is reminiscent of his birthplace in Andalucia, southern Spain.

The circus troupe is assembled as if departing, both literally and metaphorically, in terms of Picasso's development. Picasso is again Harlequin, holding the little girl, possibly his beloved younger sister, Conchita, whose tragic death from diphtheria at the age of seven affected Picasso deeply. He bargained that he would never paint again if she survived, so her death created his first obsessive, recurrent connection between art, life and death in his work. The paunchy jester is the Symbolist Apollinaire, and the older boy-acrobat is either the poet Max Jacob or the poet André Salmon. Picasso's lover of the time, Fernande, is probably the woman strangely separated from the group.

The fresco-like colours create the haunting mood of this deserted landscape, a dislocated pastoral scene emptied of life except for the figures, and also oddly separated from the traditional 'big-top' setting.

THE JESTER (1905)

Courtesy of Christie's Images

WHILE he was working on his circus studies, Picasso attempted his first major foray into sculpture with this jester's head cast in bronze. The work was cast by Vollard and the head was based on his wild, comic friend, the homosexual poet Max Jacob. After the two men returned from the famous Cirque Medrano one night, Picasso modelled a bare head using clay; it was gradually modified with the inclusion of the definitive hat. In fact, the shape and style of the jester's hat surfaces in several works including the massive *Saltimbanques*, in which it is worn by Picasso's other court jester from his bohemian troupe, the French symbolist poet Apollinaire, who also plundered the circus tradition for a series of poems on Harlequinnade.

Saltimbanques (The Family of Saltimbanques) (1905)
Chester Dale Collection. Courtesy of the National Gallery of Art, Washington D.C./Bob Grove. (See p. 50)

The Cirque Medrano was guardian of the entertainment tradition in La Pigalle, still Paris's theatre-land and home to nightclubs today. Picasso's images of this famous show had already been well celebrated by painters such Degas, Seurat and Toulouse-Lautrec.

The impetus for this crude bronze probably came during work on the *Young Acrobat on a Ball* (1905), whose dynamic movement was possibly modelled from a Goetz bronze, *Boy Balancing on a Ball*. A live model would not have been able to hold the pose for long enough.

BOY WITH A FRILLED COLLAR (1905)

Courtesy of Christie's Images

WITH his tight harlequin-style hat, this figure has evolved out of the circus imagery from Picasso's late Rose Period. Worked in gouache on cardboard, the fine, winsome face and awkward tapering Mannerist hands are still reminiscent of early characters, like the portrait of Sabartés, yet a certain finesse is more apparent. Although the hand seems oddly misshapen and exaggerated, the medium seemed to encourage a delicacy as Picasso experimented with the achievable effects of this new colouring. However, even though the pallet is much warmer, the artist has deliberately restricted his use of colour.

At this point Picasso had returned from a short stay in Holland during the early summer of 1905. He was obviously stirred by the statuesque Dutch women with their more rounded shape and rosier skins. The anorexic gamins were gradually abandoned and a more Rubens-esque development commenced in Picasso's female forms. However, this is balanced by the introduction of the lithe male juvenile shape, as shown here. The theme of the more fluid adolescent form is one that Picasso explored when he moved, with Fernande, to the Spanish Andorran retreat of Gósol for a few months during the following summer.

Sabartés (Le Bock or Glass of Beer) (1901)
Pushkin Museum, Moscow. Courtesy of Art Resource.
(See p. 22)

GÓSOL (1906)

Courtesy of Christie's Images

AFTER years of painting tortured characters, nudes and the odd pastoral scene, the intensity of this landscape is striking. Suddenly we are faced with the full force of Picasso's passion – possibly last seen with the *Bullfight* picture of 1901 – as vibrant reds, oranges and excited brushwork explode into action.

Gósol is undoubtedly a turning point in Picasso's career in that the break from the heady bohemian artistic fervour of Paris allowed the Spaniard to rediscover his heritage in this tiny peasant village, high in the Pyrenées. Beauty, in terms of appreciation of nature, is recaptured during this interlude away from the sordid, squalid city life in Montmartre. Simplistic values return as well as a lost *joie de vivre*. The desire to show Spain to Fernande, 2,000 francs in his pocket from Vollard for the Rose Period figures and a healthy lifestyle all contributed to Picasso's well-being. Gósol is primitive, inaccessible except by donkey, but most of all, it is beautiful.

Workbooks of the time reveal that Picasso dabbled with experimental prototypes for sculpture, pottery, still lifes and even uncharacteristic flower paintings – though many of these were not completed. Gósol was an artistic laboratory from which the revolutionary *Les Demoiselles d'Avignon* (1907) and ensuing Cubist movement were probably born.

ADOLESCENTS (1906)

Orangerie, Paris. Courtesy of Giraudon

*T*HESE adolescent figures were either executed in Gósol or on Picasso's return to Paris. They certainly follow the style of the other young male studies that he completed at the village, some in pencil, charcoal and gouache. This painting is oil on canvas but it has an almost a Greco-Roman aura with its ochre tonality, the plastery, mural effects and the figures' poses, which are seen again in *Les Demoiselles d'Avignon* (1907). Again, the work is more a study of colour and its tonal effects rather than a true exploration of form, but a journey into art history has begun which could be seen to end with the studied primitivism of *Les Demoiselles d'Avignon*.

The influence of Gauguin's quest into primitivism is noticeable in the heavy body shape of the figures, similar to Gauguin's South Sea Island native figures, yet Matisse's flowing Fauvist lines can also be detected around the bodies. Fauvism had just hit Paris, and Picasso was renowned for an eclectic adaptation of styles, although he never became a follower of this movement. He met Matisse, who was showing his celebrated *Bonheur de Vivre* at the Salon des Indépendants, earlier that year through his famous patron Gertrude Stein. However, as the two painters both developed into great artists, their relationship was often to be competitive.

Les Demoiselles d'Avignon (1907)
The Museum of Modern Art, New York. Acquired through the Lillie P. Bliss Bequest. Courtesy of the Museum of Modern Art, New York. (See p. 60)

LES DEMOISELLES D'AVIGNON (1907)

The Museum of Modern Art, New York. Acquired through the Lillie P. Bliss Bequest.
Courtesy of the Museum of Modern Art, New York

*C*ALLED the most innovative painting since the work of
Giotto, when *Les Demoiselles d'Avignon* first appeared it was
as if the art world had collapsed. Known form and
representation were completely abandoned. The reductionism and
contortion of space in the painting were incredible, and the
dislocation of faces explosive. Like any revolution, the shock
waves reverberated and the inevitable outcome was Cubism.

This large work, which took nine months to complete,
exposes the true genius and novelty of Picasso's passion. Suddenly
he found freedom of expression away from current and classical
French influences and was able to carve his own path – his own
movement, like that of his friend and rival Matisse – which he
dubbed 'an exorcism'. Whereas Matisse was left to explore colour,
Picasso opened up the experimental field of form, which then
became his life-long devotion.

Commentators point to Cézanne's monumental nudes in
The Bathers series and the impact of African art on Western art as
influences on this painting. However, Picasso also explores
Gauguin's primitivism with the inclusion of features taken from
ancient Iberian facemasks. The gradual rounding of Fernande's
shape away from the anorexic models of the Blue and Rose
periods also climaxes here – but the violent sexuality of these
twisted nudes in their brothel setting is disturbing.

SELF-PORTRAIT (1907)

Prague National Gallery. Courtesy of Giraudon

*T*HE savage painting technique of *Les Demoiselles d'Avignon* (1907) is expanded further in this self-portrait with its heavy striation and angular structure. The painting was completed during the working of *Les Demoiselles d'Avignon*, while Picasso took a break from the evolving epic piece, which at this stage featured two male figures, a sailor and medical student. These were later painted out in the final work to leave the celebrated female nude group.

This self-portrait is interesting as an early development of the final primitive mask-like form in *Les Demoiselles d'Avignon*. Picasso apparently bought two primitive Iberian sculptured heads from Apollinaire's secretary early that year. These had been stolen from the Louvre in Paris. A study of the sculptures no doubt influenced many works of this period, including this portrait, whose features have a distinct three-dimensional sculptural quality.

The picture's child-like air is significant, with the emphasis on the staring, almost vacant aspect of the eyes, a fascination revisited in final works such as *Profile of a Woman's Face* (1960). There is a passionate sensuality about this younger, happier face compared to earlier self-portraits, though an intensity of look is palpable due to the hatching and harshly contrasting colours, which combine to create a vivid consolidation of energy.

Profile of a Woman's Face (1960)
Courtesy of Christie's Images. (See p. 226)

SEATED NUDE (1910)
Courtesy of the Tate Gallery

*T*HE final collapse of form into Cubism, from *Les Demoiselles d'Avignon* (1907) to this work, was gradual and Picasso was greatly influenced by what he called his 'marriage' with fellow experimenter, French artist Georges Braque. Braque's rigid disciplinarian approach helped to stabilise Picasso's development, which had gone astray after the *Demoiselles* masterpiece.

Seated Nude is part of a series from late 1909 to spring 1910, and a summation of earlier Cubist three-dimensional experimental work on still life and portraits. In fact, this time of experiment and research gives this period the title of Analytical Cubism, with its manipulation and fragmentation of space and multiple angles of vision. Picasso's whole preoccupation with the notion of vision, explored in the earlier blind man images, now finds its thematic challenge in Cubism.

In this picture, the female form is a blur; yet although the traditional representational form has collapsed we still discern its shape as Picasso studies the relationship of the figure to its surrounding space. The development of 'passages', connecting areas of spatial coherence, involves a remarkable complexity and balance between total abstraction of pictorial signs and recognisable features, especially with the return of an almost monochromatic palette similar to *Woman in a Chemise* (1905) from the late Blue Period.

Woman in a Chemise (1905*)*
Courtesy of the Tate Gallery.
(See p. 42)

CATALANE (C. 1910–11)

Courtesy of Christie's Images

IN the midst of Picasso's artistic journey into the analytical Cubist world of spatial distortion, this sketch provides an odd, amusing interlude and is probably a forerunner of his later aesthetic forays in to art as a political statement.

During his summer stay with Fernande in 1909 in Catalonia, Spain, a revolutionary uprising in the region's capital, Barcelona, Picasso's main home, transformed into a general strike, with the army killing 175 workers and arresting 2000. Violent repression ended any attempts at what Picasso called the quest for 'a new Spain', which resurfaced so significantly with the Spanish Civil War (1936–38), immortalised forever in Picasso's stunning political retort, *Guernica* (1937).

Fernande was probably the model for this symbolic Catalonian 'worker' peasant-woman carrying a palm of peace. The palm tree appears in several other early Cubist landscapes painted during this period. The date of this work is uncertain, probably between late 1910 and 1911, when Picasso is said to have discarded many old approaches and started with new figurations.

Here, the wonderfully expressive freedom of movement and colour not only recalls the ground-breaking background sketch-work to *Les Demoiselles d'Avignon* (1907) but the childlike naiveté of line heralds the devastating, simplistic power of *Guernica* 27 years later.

Guernica (1937)
The Prado, Madrid. Courtesy of Giraudon. (See p. 148)

THE FAN (L'INDÉPENDENT) (1911)

Courtesy of Christie's Images

AT THIS point, Cubism had developed a new pictorial language with the introduction of lettering and iconographic devices known as 'identification keys'. *The Fan* was painted in Céret in the French Pyrenées in the summer of 1911. Picasso stayed there without Fernande as their relationship was disintegrating, and he was joined briefly by Braque. In this picture, the local newspaper title is reproduced with Gothic lettering, a device first developed by Braque to emphasis the Cubist ambiguities of shallow pictorial surface and depth.

However, the loosening of the blue palette allows a wonderful movement to fill this work. The warmer yellowy ochres, reminiscent of *Gósol* (1906), represent a significant colour shift as if the sunnier southern climate again influenced Picasso's sense of well-being and his artistic mood. This freedom of movement is expressed beautifully as the space opens up gradually like the opening of a fan but in a series of Cubist spatial displacements.

The effect is achieved by an overall centred diamond pattern, which has been constructed from the echoing fan-like structures, spreading out from the fan's defined axis point just above the newspaper heading. This diamond configuration is bound at the sides by a circular motion, implying further movement of the dislocated fan.

Gósol (1906)
Courtesy of Christie's Images. (See p. 56)

WOMAN ON THE GUITAR (MA JOLIE) (1911)

Acquired through the Lillie P. Bliss Bequest. Courtesy of the Museum of Modern Art, New York

*H*ERE the development of lettering evolves as a complex system of messages, puns and private references. 'Ma Jolie' was a popular song of the time and was Picasso's fond semiotic reference to the new love in his life, Eva Gouel, (Marcelle Humbert), the mistress of a fellow Polish artist. They met at the home of Picasso's chief patron, Gertrude Stein, and Picasso was completely smitten. Eva died tragically in 1915 after a short illness.

There is confusion concerning dating of this work, however the signage and distinct pyramidal structure are critical in suggesting the winter of 1911. The interplay between the female figure and instrument is constructed into the overall pyramidal form, using a complex system of light and shade to create a kaleidoscopic effect.

This work is again part of a series of figures and musical instruments, as Picasso attempts to develop notions of lyricism within the tight confines of heavily angular space. The figure is somehow liberated from the gridlines of the surrounding space, whereas the slanting lines, implying the disrupted form and space of the guitar, establish a dynamic diagonal counter tension. A similar artistic theme is re-explored in the radically surreal *Three Dancers* (1925). As his friend Apollinaire famously said, 'Picasso was re-ordering the universe'.

The Three Dancers (1925)
Courtesy of the Tate Gallery, London. (See p. 116)

MAN WITH A GUITAR (1911)

Picasso Museum, Paris. Courtesy of Giraudon

The Three Musicians (1921)
The Museum of Modern Art, New York. Mrs Simon Guggenheim Fund.
Courtesy of the Museum of Modern Art, New York. (See p. 104)

AGAIN the gradual loosening of form – from the tight spatial restrictions of high analytical Cubism – is beginning to be felt here. The pyramidal structure is in place but the heavy geometrical shapes are allowed a gentler, more rhythmical feel, counterbalanced by the swirling column-like shape at the bottom, denoting the picture's base. The repeated darkened shape also echoes the guitar, which is more clearly represented this time as a recognised form in the centre of the picture. It makes a full appearance at the height of Synthetic Cubism in *The Three Musicians* (1921).

Here, the use of shading and contrasting ochre against the blue further emphasises this strong section, almost lifting it from the picture plane as if the lyrical resonance of the guitar is giving the picture sensory life. The inclusion of a wineglass in the top right, the lettering KOU – slashed by a horizontal line to create spatial depth – and the notion that this is a corner of a room, suggest a café scene, as in a work by Braque called *The Portuguese.*

MANDOLIN (C. 1911)

Courtesy of Christie's Images

A GREY wash on paper, this is a working study for the profusion of Cubist works featuring musical instruments, which became increasingly prevalent as the intense exploratory nature of the analytical period gave way to the visually easier and more schematic approach of Synthetic Cubism. The delicacy of the wash helped to produce a lighter, lyrical feel even though the distortion of the instrument's shape is still apparent. The armature of the shape is still clearly defined, while the close detail of the mandolin's neck captures the tension in the tightly stretched strings.

The simple reductionist elements of this drawing allowed Picasso to analyse the fundamental aspects of the instrument's form that would be required to generate meaning. The removal of most features except for the stringed neck and the traditional, recognisable bowing of the mandolin body leave the essence of the form in tact.

This research is invaluable for Picasso's next move into Cubist sculpture which explored the relationship between volume, form and significant meaning. As a result, aspects of this wash can be identified in the later series, such as in *Mandolin and Clarinet* (1913), where this string formation is repeated in simple blue paint on the mandolin's wooden framed neck.

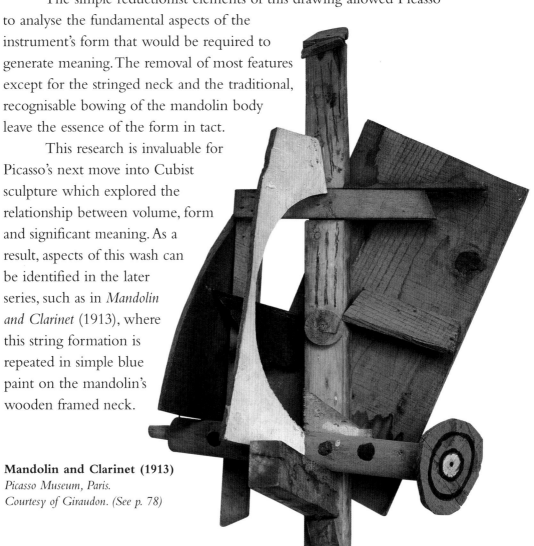

Mandolin and Clarinet (1913)
Picasso Museum, Paris.
Courtesy of Giraudon. (See p. 78)

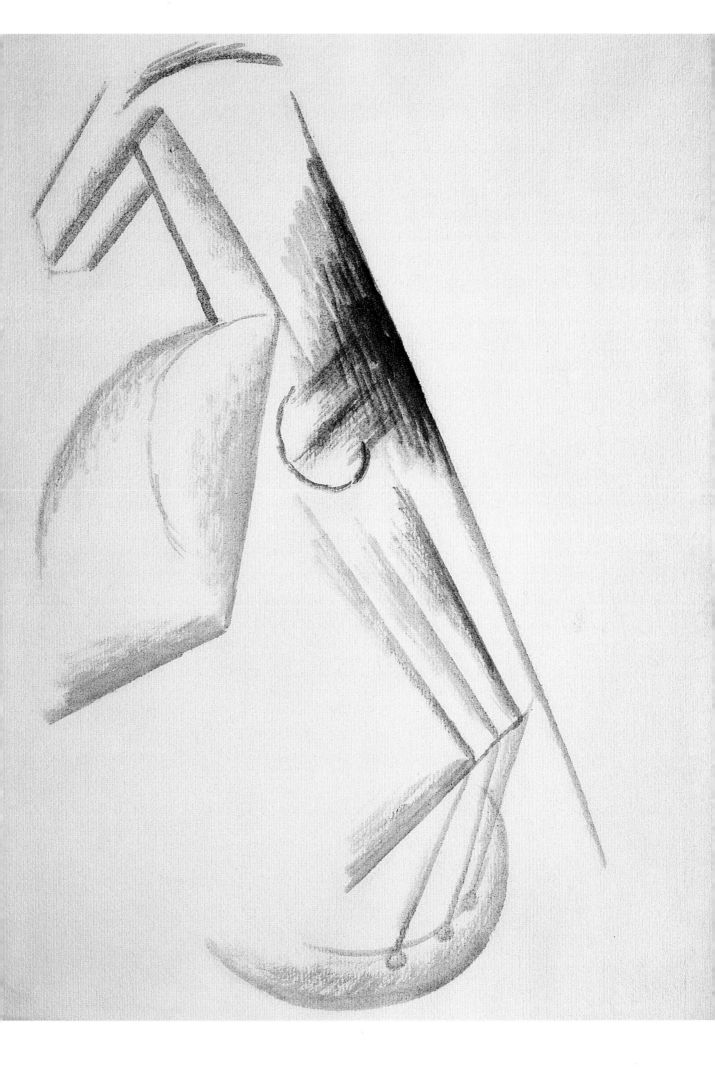

VIOLIN, BOTTLE AND GLASS (1913)
Courtesy of Christie's Images

*T*HE inclusion of lettering now progresses to the revolutionary introduction of collage and papiers-collés during this period as the development of form and space allows more freedom of movement. From a new Paris studio, Picasso worked intensely during 1912 and into 1913 on images of musical instruments and other still-life objects, incorporating musical scores, newspapers and pasted papers, and using an amazing variety of media, such as gouache, pencil, charcoal and sand on paper or canvas. This particular work from early 1913 is a combination of oil and pasted papers on canvas.

The rhythm of the violin form, separated and locked into vertical bands, is disrupted by the return of Picasso's recurrent diamond shape, this time implied in the pattern of the orange wallpaper, painted bottom left, and a copy of actual wallpaper used in similar earlier works of this period. The letters top right are cut from a newspaper and the trompe-l'oeil technique on the pipe and the JOB cigarette papers are a new development. The theme is developed further in *Still Life: The Violin* (1914).

This inclusion of house decorators' techniques is said to be due to Braque's continuing influence upon Picasso – he was once a house painter – as the artists explored the modernist bricolage world of inter-linking texture and colour.

Still Life: The Violin (1914)
Gallery of Modern Art, Paris. Courtesy of Topham. (See p. 80)

MANDOLIN AND CLARINET (1913)

Picasso Museum, Paris. Courtesy of Giraudon

*T*HE Cubist sculpture was the next logical development after the introduction of collage and pasted shapes, with their intrinsic impression of volume. Picasso was fascinated by the absorption of a foreign body or raw material within a painted surface and sculpture continued this exploration.

This particular work is again a culmination of a number of similar constructions. Here the main medium is wood with the arc of a circle cut from a perpendicular plank, painted white, to denote the body of the mandolin. The remaining cut-out is painted blue and fixed to the side. The strings and central hole are discernible on the gently whitened neck of the instrument. The clarinet is the simple structure cutting the bottom of the work, crudely painted with blue holes.

Although Braque had earlier played with cardboard models to assist in the construction of his paintings, the first Cubist sculpture is seen as Picasso's *The Guitar* of 1912. As Picasso expert Timothy Hilton notes, this new sculptural method marks the revolutionary development of construction rather than the traditional inductive or reductive methods of modelling and carving. Its impact is felt on the rest of the twentieth century, as well as in his own later Synthetic Cubist works, such as *Man before a Fireplace* (1916).

Man before a Fireplace (1916)
Picasso Museum, Paris. Courtesy of Giraudon. (See p. 86)

STILL LIFE: THE VIOLIN (1914)

Gallery of Modern Art, Paris. Courtesy of Topham

FINALLY the early Cubist restraints on space and form, as in *Woman on the Guitar (Ma Jolie)* (1911), become relaxed following the introduction of collage and papiers-collés. They allow the return of a more representational phase, known as Synthetic Cubism. This sees the welding of abstract elements into a representational whole, which eventually progressed to Surrealism by the end of the decade.

For Picasso this is a remarkably fertile and poetic period as whole new worlds are recreated out of everyday objects. 'Synthesis' means that the objects do not imitate life but create their own meaning – so a newspaper cutting can become a bottle, in turn questioning the accepted linguistic values of both items. As Picasso states, 'we tried to get rid of trompe d'oeil for trompe d'esprit' … a displaced object enters a universe for which it was not made and where it retains, in a measure, its strangeness.

This work sees the profusion of iconography and symbolism from other oeuvres, with the dislocated planes of the guitar, bottle of Bass, the clarinet, violin and ace of clubs, all locked in by an overlapping series of Pointillist squares, which re-introduce a delicate mottled world of colour. In fact the papiers-collés solved the Cubist's problem of how to re-establish colour.

Woman on the Guitar (Ma Jolie) (1911)
The Museum of Modern Art, New York. Acquired through the Lillie P. Bliss Bequest. Courtesy of the Museum of Modern Art, New York. (See p. 70)

THE ARTIST AND HIS MODEL (1914)

Picasso Museum, Paris. Courtesy of Giraudon

*T*HIS painting is an amazing return to traditional naturalism during an intense period of Synthetic Cubism. It is often regarded as an important feature of this year's work as the unfinished canvas reveals the working drawings of a seated artist, contemplating the female model. It depicts the first systematic face since 1910 and is possibly the only face inspired by Eva, who was to die suddenly the following year.

The work was started during Picasso's Avignon period, from June to October 1914, and, like other work, is said to be unfinished because of the outbreak of the First World War. The return to naturalism indicates not only a radical change of style but of approach to subject matter. As Picasso reflects on beauty, in the form of the love of his life, there is no attempt to disfigure, distort or incorporate some misogynous social comment about prostitution or gender issues, as in *Les Demoiselles d'Avignon* (1907).

Picasso also produced a series of naturalist pencil drawings of non-artist friends, although fellow artists were stunned by this 'development', which heralded his later move into neo-Classicism as in *Woman's Head* (1921). Once again he reveals his versatility of spirit and refusal to be trapped by any one movement or style after it has outlived its creative purpose.

Woman's Head (1921)
Courtesy of Christie's Images. (See p. 100)

MAN IN A BOWLER HAT, SEATED IN AN ARMCHAIR (MAN WITH A PIPE) (1915)

Chicago Art Institute. Courtesy of Topham

*T*HE year 1915 was a sombre one, with the impact of World War One being felt in France and most men joining up, including Georges Braque (1882–1963), who was seriously injured, and fellow painter André Derain (1880–1954). Picasso was viewed with suspicion by contemporary society as he was young and healthy yet did not go to fight; in fact he demonstrated considerable ambivalence in his attitude to the war, especially with his obvious close connections to his main art dealer, the Paris-based German, Daniel-Henry Kahnweiler.

However, this large canvas, 130 x 90 cm (52 x 36 in), has a quiet humour and feeling of composure. The use of Pointillist-style dots, with their stippled effect and the inclusion of a painted marble-effect herald Picasso's return to colour exploration and his interest in the development of interior design processes. The incorporation of frieze-like techniques, with areas of architectural scrolling, creates a sense of movement to oppose the tension of the solid piling up of the angular blocks. These techniques also connote the curling of smoke from the pipe in the bottom right of the picture. The experimental return to Naturalism filters through in this painting with the half-figurative face, hands and waistcoat fragment, though with comic intent. The artist's sense of humour is apparent in the jigsaw compilations of the face, whose bizarre, textured overlays create the nose, moustache and mouth so that a bird-shape appears. Picasso was moving away from Cubism, as seen in *Man with a Guitar* (1911). Surrealism was beckoning.

Man with a Guitar (1911)
Picasso Museum, Paris. Courtesy of Giraudon.
(See p. 72)

MAN BEFORE A FIREPLACE (1916)

Picasso Museum, Paris. Courtesy of Giraudon

SOMBRE and restrained, the desolation Picasso experienced after Eva's early death at the end of 1915 can be felt deeply in this work, which is an example of several pieces involving men or women seated or standing by a defined form, such as an armchair or fireplace. However, the gentle touch of humour of *Man in a Bowler Hat, Seated in an Armchair* (1915) is missing here.

Another large work, at 130 x 80 cm (52 x 32 in), this piece was lost and only came to light after Picasso's death when an inventory was drawn up. His recent explosions of colour are more muted here, arrested within the piled construction which forms the man's body. After recent forays into figurative work, this is a sudden plunge into almost total abstraction. The identifiable moulded, curved frame of the mirror, mantel-shelf and fire surround, better viewed at a distance, are superbly juxtaposed against the intensity of the abstract figure, throwing its form into strange relief.

During this period, Picasso was invited by the poet Jean Cocteau to design the decor for a new Ballets Russes work, *Parade*. He was also caught up in the formative Dada arts group of refugee writers and artists based in Switzerland, whose nihilistic principles eventually surfaced as political radicalism and Surrealism.

Man in a Bowler Hat, Seated in an Armchair (Man with Pipe) (1915)
Chicago Art Institute. Courtesy of Topham.
(See p. 84)

PORTRAIT OF OLGA IN AN ARMCHAIR (1917)

Picasso Museum, Paris. Courtesy of Giraudon

A RETURN to Picasso's Spanish roots is significant with this stunning figurative portrait of the Ballets Russes ballerina, Olga Koklova, soon to become his first wife. As with his previous lovers, Fernande and Eva, he reinstates traditional realistic, aesthetic methods to contemplate beauty and its relationship to art.

Here, Olga serenely sits with a marmoreal, doll-like face looking down wistfully at the viewer. The wonderfully painted backdrop of the chair and the colourful, half-opened fan mitigates the severity of the black clothing and tight black hair. The blue shading around Olga's form, which throws her further into stark relief, almost seems unfinished as with the blue background that haloes around Eva in *The Artist and his Model* (1914).

Picasso's involvement with Olga and the Ballet Russes revolutionised his life style as he started to mix with high society, following the troupe around Europe. When Apollinaire finally married in spring 1918, Picasso was inspired and married Olga in July. They honeymooned in Biarritz, feted by this social centre of aristocracy and beautiful people, and returned to Paris late September where they moved into a house in a glamorous district. The sudden death of Apollinaire from flu two days before Armistice Day shocked the arts world.

The Artist and his Model (1914)
Picasso Museum, Paris. Courtesy of Giraudon. (See p. 82)

THE BATHERS (1918)

Picasso Museum, Paris. Courtesy of Giraudon

*T*HIS strange picture, painted while Picasso and Olga were honeymooning at Biarritz, is a forerunner of the monumental neo-Classical and Surrealist bodies, like *The Kiss* (1931), soon to play on Picassoan beaches over the next few years. Picasso's own carefree mood of personal happiness, no doubt contributed to this continuing break from Cubism and the suggestion of Romanticism.

The exaggerated bright colours of the bathing costumes accentuate the women's elongated shapes, reminiscent of Picasso's earlier explorations of late sixteenth-century Italian Mannerists. The rhythmical curves of these bodies deliberately create an oppositional tension to the perpendicular lines of the lighthouse, seashore and horizon. The sway of the standing woman, with the carefree, voluptuous freeing of her hair, is echoed in the wind-filled shape of the yacht's sail. However, despite the scene's apparent frivolity, the backdrop's colouring is subdued and ghostly, with the grey tones of the beach and chilly aquamarine of the sea reflected thinly in the sky tones.

Preliminary drawings also reveal the painting's indebtedness to the nineteenth-century French artist Ingres, whose influence was noticeable in Picasso's early works but had been abandoned with the march into Cubism. In his art, Ingres sought to reconcile a searching truth with the inescapable romanticism of his time. This was expressed, as Picasso expresses it here, in silhouette, by purity of line and relief-like modelling.

**Figures at the Seaside (1931)
(The Kiss)**
Picasso Museum, Paris. Courtesy of Giraudon.
(See p. 124)

THE LOVERS (1919)

Musée Picasso, Paris. Courtesy of the Picasso Administration / Photo RMN–R.G. Ojeda

THE red passion and sexual energy of this work explodes on the canvas as the dancing lovers take up a beautiful rhythm. As with the *Man in a Bowler Hat, Seated in an Armchair* (1915) there is a wonderful underlying sense of humour with the figures' displaced faces, similarly formed by jigsaw cut-outs.

Picasso no longer seemed haunted by issues of space, depth and colour but how to secure reality. It was time to apply the past 20 years of artistic exploration in a new direction. There was a sense of freedom to go forwards. The war was over and he was settled domestically; he was famous and he was financially comfortable.

Here, the dancers represent a return to the Commedia dell'Arte sequence of harlequin and pierrot characters, no doubt inspired by his continuing association, through new wife Olga, with the ballet and theatre scene; during 1919 he worked with the Ballet Russes in London. However, in this work, apart from the suggestion of a clown-like bobble hat, the couple appear smartly dressed while poised in an embrace or dance hold. The woman's fashionable shorter dress length and dinner jacket-style suit of the male figure underlines their connections, like Picasso's, with fashionable high society. Braque, like other friends, disapproved strongly of Picasso's new-found socialite friends, as well as his new style of art.

Man in a Bowler Hat, Seated in an Armchair (Man with a Pipe) (1915)
Chicago Art Institute. Courtesy of Topham. (See p. 84)

STILL LIFE OF A PIGEON (1919)

Courtesy of Christie's Images

*D*URING 1919 and 1920, Picasso slipped easily between Cubism and his rediscovered naturalism, to the chagrin of those who felt he had betrayed much of what the Cubist revolution had laboured to create. As others marched towards abstraction, Picasso's artistic pluralism allowed him to seek the best form of expression for whatever he was working on at the time. This resulted in a wonderful series of still-lifes during this period, including this work, which were planned for a major exhibition in Paris in the autumn.

Picasso later argued that the two artistic idioms were complementary and therefore interchangeable, enabling him to explore an effective relationship between them, as here and in the previous work, *The Lovers* (1919). Here, too, he tackles Cubist issues of space, depth and colour, but in order to secure reality, as wonderful textures elegantly tumble from the canvas. The kitchen table is realistically defined, as is the form of the pigeon, with its naturalistic wings and feathers that correspond to the surrounding patterning. However, the Cubist fracturing of the bird's bodily sections across the table enables Picasso to project a tremendous concept of dynamism into the dead bird's neck, which hangs over the table creating a sense of life in death.

Woman Sitting on a Couch (1920)

Courtesy of Christie's Images

*H*ERE, Picasso has moved back into the Cubist world of fractured space and dislocation to paint a theme that recurs throughout his career, so much so that elements of this work are unmistakably evident, for instance, in the freer, looser Surrealist work of *Nude Woman in Red Armchair* (1932). Picasso possibly returned to study this particular earlier work again.

At this point in his career, Picasso is obviously enjoying his new-found artistic freedom and the ability to move, as the work demanded, from Cubism to naturalism, or to incorporate techniques from both. However, this work is almost completely Cubist, with few 'keys' to the meaning. Its title assists the viewer as we gradually discern the structure of the chair, the casual whitened-out arm of the sitter resting on the chair top, and the exaggerated sweeping movement of the other pink arm, whose blue fist rests in her lap. The round pumpkin-like shape of the blue head certainly seems to pre-figure the full curves of the 1932 model.

The exaggerated circular movement of the pink arm, contrasting with the heavy linear segments, may be significant, possibly denoting Olga's pregnant shape, as she was expecting Picasso's first son, Paulo, at the time.

Nude Woman in Red Armchair (1932)
Courtesy of the Tate Gallery. (See p. 132)

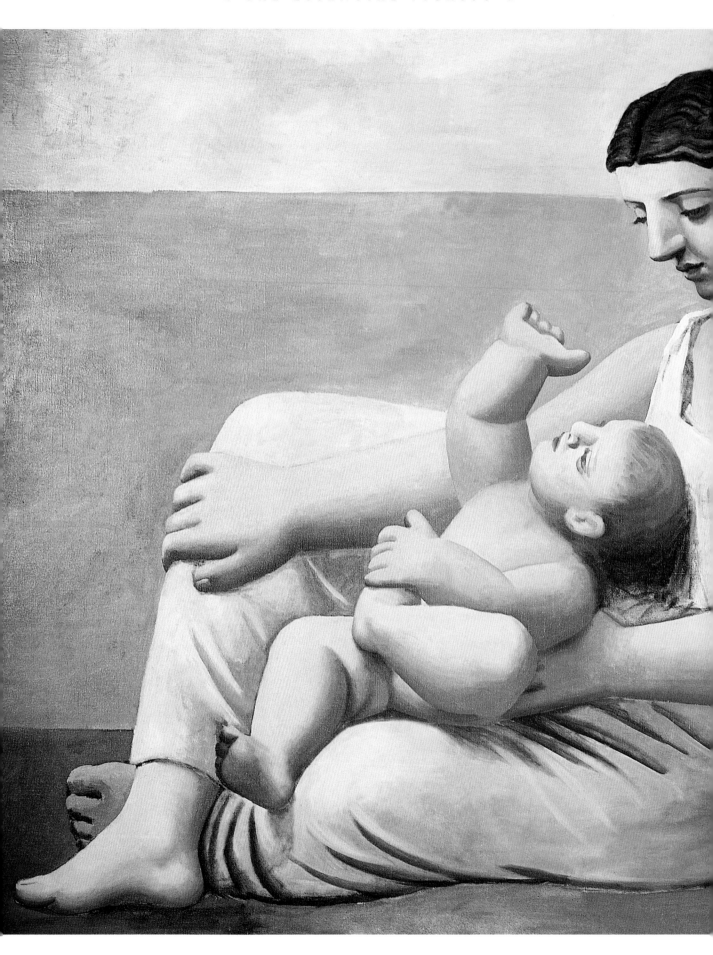

MOTHER AND CHILD (1921)
Chicago Art Institute. Courtesy of Topham

THE rounded monumental figures of Picasso's neo-Classical period of the early 1920s sees a return to his favourite, emotionally charged theme of mother and child, with all its traditional religious connotations. Neo-Classicism originally applies to the late eighteenth- and early nineteenth-century revival of Classical motifs, subjects and decorations, with the inspiration coming from the 1748 excavations of Pompeii and writings of the German archaeologist, Wincklemann. Picasso visited Pompeii and some Italian museums of Classical art in 1917, and their influence began to assert itself in this post-war series of colossal figures. A general reaction against the pre-war excesses and violent origins of Cubism and Expressionism saw a popular desire in art for the order, rationalised structure and humanity represented by this eighteenth-century movement.

The statuesque proportions of the mother and child in this large five-foot square canvas are set intimately against an almost colourless beach backdrop. This bold Mannerist style of figuration, either elongated or, as here, enlarged and forced into the composition, is echoed in other works of this era.

A return to the mother and child theme, this time in a more composed and contented mood, could be due to the birth of Picasso's first child, Paulo, in February 1921.

WOMAN'S HEAD (1921)

Courtesy of Christie's Images

ONCE again the colossal monumentalism of the neo-Classical revival can be seen in this large female head, reminiscent of Pompeian frescoes and Renaissance painting. However, the almost sculptured profile with the Classical nose and well-defined eye regions is mitigated by suggestions of Picasso's earlier primitivism explorations of 1906–07, as seen in the solid neck, rounded jaw and implied corpulence of the body. This primitive, earthy chubbiness suggests sensual life within the statuesque frame.

Mother and Child (1921)
Chicago Art Institute.
Courtesy of Topham. (See p. 98)

Picasso continues to work in subdued colours as he experiments with the form and style of the period. The pale blue-grey hues of *Mother and Child* (1921) are strengthened here into emphatic colours. The distinct blues deliberately throw the head into sharp relief, stressing its monumental profile. Heavy and intense brushwork, particularly in the shaded areas of the neck and jaw and the background, also underline the sense of intentional primitive crudeness and simplicity.

Images of women depicted in this era have an iconic religious feel. They are early Mediterranean mythological creatures or crude and simple Madonna representations rather than the imminent distorted and violently eroticised figures of Surrealism and beyond. Presumably this period of domestic bliss and paternal stability is reflected in the gentle rhythmical rotundity of these neo-Classical women.

THREE WOMEN AT THE FOUNTAIN (SPRING) (1921)

The Museum of Modern Art, New York. Gift of Mr and Mrs Allan D. Emil. Courtesy of the Museum of Modern Art, New York

THIS wonderful picture's primitive, early Mediterranean feel is another vibrant example of Picasso's monumental neo-Classical figures. The three women emerge from the rocky scene like gigantic sculptures in relief, their strong chiselled profiles and exaggerated statuesque contours reminiscent of late or provincial Hellenistic styles, from the time of Alexander the Great's successors. The massive work is 204 x 174 cm (7 x 5.5 ft) in size, and its perspective draws the viewer's eye up to these huge shapes.

The strange rotundity of the bodies is not only juxtaposed by the heavily hewed faces but by the deep gouged-in lines to denote the folds of the dresses. The accentuated width of these folds and the dramatic use of colour to create them – silvery in quality, against the bright blue – add to this sense of heightened relief, contrasting with the browny ochre backdrop of the rocks.

This use of folding to create motion and define shape is similar to techniques Picasso used in earlier pictures from the Blue Period, such as *Mother and Child (Maternity)* (1901). Here, instead of creating a rhythm to counteract the strong perpendicular lines of the chair, the folds act in reverse, creating a heavy, angular tension.

Mother and Child (Maternity) (1901)
Courtesy of Topham. (See p. 26)

THE THREE MUSICIANS (1921)

The Museum of Modern Art, New York. Mrs Simon Guggenheim Fund.
Courtesy of the Museum of Modern Art, New York

THIS celebrated work, now in the New York Museum of Modern Art, is part of series painted while Picasso was with his young family in Fontainebleau in the summer of 1921. It marks a return to high Synthetic Cubism and his enduring Commedia dell'Arte imagery, commenced in the early days in Paris. His continuing association with the refined world of ballet, through his wife and through his work designing sets and costumes for Diaghilev, is evident throughout.

Again, like *The Lovers* (1919), there is a wonderful sense of humour in the work, even though the masked cut-out overlays of the three faces, and the intense white blocking give the figures a sinister appearance. Unlike the early synthetic papiers-collés with their realist inclusion of sheet music, the notes here are iconographic to the point of being cartoonesque. The crudely shaped clarinet is a repetition of his early Cubist sculpture, *Mandolin and Clarinet* (1913) and no doubt the centred harlequin with his boldly coloured, exaggerated costume is Picasso, leader of this strange musical band. This harlequin, like Picasso, is the magician of his art, conjuring up mystical sounds; his musical notes, like Picasso's no doubt, resonating at an eccentric modernist pitch.

Mandolin and Clarinet (1913)
Picasso Museum, Paris. Courtesy of Giraudon. (See p. 79)

THE LARGE BATHER (1921)
Courtesy of Art Resource / Erich Lessing

*P*ICASSO'S obsession with Monumentalism continued as he further explored how to create a dynamic oppositional tension between the heavy solidity of the roughly hewn Neo-Classical body shape, which appears here crammed into the confines of the picture frame, and the apparent movement of the undulating folds of fabric. Again, the folds are heavily exaggerated and formed from a dramatic use of colour, this time a verdant green edged with silver, to add to the heightened sense of relief. This static-motion polarisation is explored within a gargantuan framework as Picasso shifts Cubist preoccupations with space definition on to a grander scale.

Despite the mammoth proportions, the huge nude exudes a primitive sensuality, recalling the artist's earlier tribal-like nude experiments of 1906-1907 in the build up to the revolutionary work *Les Demoiselles d'Avignon* (1907). Yet somehow the gigantic head, with its wistful expression, long classical nose and heavily defined eyes, recalls some of Picasso's superbly sensitive drawings of Fernande, also from the innovative 1906 period during their idyllic time at Gósol. This sensitivity, reiterated as the giantess demurely covers her pubic region with the fabric's folds, is another of the many superb dichotomies at work in these monumental studies, in which Picasso challenges our accepted concepts of female beauty wonderfully.

La Belle Fernande (1906)
Courtesy of Christie's Images. (See p. 44)

THE BIRD CAGE (1923)

Courtesy of Topham

*T*HIS bright, animated work marks the transition from the layered, textural approach of high Synthetic Cubism to the looser free flowing expressions of Picasso's Surrealist period.

Oil and charcoal on canvas, *The Bird Cage* has tight, geometric structures and a kaleidoscopic fracturing of the central image, but instead of the placement of identity 'keys' – pictorial representations of reality within the dislocated Cubist world – the images are in an almost surreal mode. The simple yellow bird, top left, has made a comic appearance in *Man in a Bowler Hat, Seated in an Armchair* (*Man with a Pipe*) (1915). Here, the bird is presumably inside the cage, though the perspective is reversed so that we are also inside with the bird, looking out at the world through the bars.

Other identifiable items portrayed in this absurd scene include patchwork fruit on a bizarre table cloth and a series of railing motifs, signifying that perhaps this cage sits on a table by a balcony.

The most dramatic transformation is the profusion of splendid colour, similar to southern Mediterranean mosaics or tiling. The bright intensity is stunning, making the picture sing with life. The bird might be only symbolically caged, but Picasso's exploration of colour is now truly unleashed.

Man in a Bowler Hat, Seated in an Armchair (Man with a Pipe) (1915)
Courtesy of Topham. (See p. 84)

THE PAN PIPES (1923)

Picasso Museum, Paris. Courtesy of Giraudon

*P*ICASSO returns to monumentalism with this gigantic work, measuring 205 cm x 174.5 cm (7 x 5.5 ft). The size of the canvas enforces the immense statuesque proportions of the figures. Like the earlier *Three Women at the Fountain (Spring)* (1921) these male figures appear to have been carved like Classical Homeric statues from the hunks of stone behind them and then imbued with life, possibly by the music from the magical pan pipes. The thin black lines around their frame and shadowing helps lift them off the picture surface to complete the sense of chiselled separation.

Pan, an ancient Greek god and patron of pastoral poets, was also a symbol of fertility and love. He played his reed pipes, formed from a nymph who metamorphosed to escape his amorous clutches. Pan was said to be dangerous in the midday heat, as represented so intensely in this picture; the deep heat emanates from the fierce blue colours in three horizontal bands.

This work sees a development of Picasso's life-long artistic fascination with male sexuality wrapped in images from mythology. The face on the left recalls earlier self-projections, such as *Self-Portrait* (1907), and suggests the 42-year-old artist's contentment with his own creativity and virility.

Self-Portrait (1907)
Prague National Gallery. Courtesy of Giraudon.
(See p. 62)

HARLEQUIN (1923)

Gallery of Modern Art, Paris. Courtesy of Topham

*T*HIS painting is actually a portrait of the Catalan painter Jacinto Salvado, who is depicted wearing a costume from a ballet production that the writer Jean Cocteau had left behind in Picasso's Parisian studio in 1916.

Picasso painted a series of harlequin portraits, many in the neo-Classic style of Salvado. As always, the theme is the concept of artist as joker, magician and creative entertainer. The fine lines and areas of colouring on the left shoulder suggest it is unfinished. Another work painted at the same time, using a side profile of Salvado, shows the full

splendour of this rose, yellow and blue costume, complete with beading, to create the traditional harlequin diamond shapes on the outfit. However, here the continuation of the texture of the hat into the jacket around the collar and under the patterning suggests that Picasso might have been developing another colour theme which he then abandoned.

It is interesting to note that Picasso, himself usually playing the role of harlequin, returns to the theme the following year with the portrait of his young son, Paulo, in a similar pose to Salvado, both holding their hands and looking out to the right.

Paulo Picasso (1924)
Picasso Museum, Paris. Courtesy of Giraudon. (See p. 114)

PAULO PICASSO (1924)

Picasso Museum, Paris. Courtesy of Giraudon

*T*HIS portrait, like that of Olga, Paulo's mother, painted in Spanish-style costume in 1917, provides an interesting note of sentimentality in Picasso's career. It is as though a return to naturalism is an interlude in which to recoup and play with the naturalist and figurative techniques of the Old Masters before advancing to the next development.

Here, the boy is dressed as the young pretender, baby harlequin, a literal and metaphorical replica of the artistic master. In fact this work is one of a series of the young boy, sometimes dressed as Pierrot, riding a donkey and even painting, all lovingly capturing the beautiful round face and dramatic eyes inherited from his mother. As he sits demurely poised on the chair, we can wonder if the portrait was completed with the assistance of photographs, as it would have been almost impossible for a child of this age to sit still for so long.

Portrait of Olga in an Armchair (1917)
Picasso Museum, Paris. Courtesy of Giraudon
(see p. 89)

Again Picasso uses the technique of a heavy background against the bright colours of the outfit to throw the boy's form into exaggerated relief. The emphasis is certainly on the harlequin costume. The fine lines of the collar and cuffs, the handkerchief and chair edging also suggest that this picture is unfinished.

THE THREE DANCERS (1925)

Courtesy of the Tate Gallery

This radical work marks Picasso's entry into Surrealism and descent into his disturbing depictions of the female form. However, he was never a fully signed up member of the Surrealism movement: his down-to-earth artistic response and individuality never truly submitted to the movement's Freudian concepts of supremacy of the subconscious state.

Yet Surrealists emerging from the Dada movement claimed Picasso as their own, with the reproduction of *Les Demoiselles d'Avignon* (1907) in their 1925 manifesto to endorse his influence on their work. *The Three Dancers* is similar to *Les Demoiselles d'Avignon* in its revolutionary impact – yet it is not the elements of primitivism but the women's psychotic frenzy that is disturbing. The bodily distortions and maniacal grimaces, combined with the figures' pyramidal structure, surface again in the equally ferocious *Crucifixion* (1930). The characters are life size, as this massive picture measures seven feet by five feet.

Critics point to Picasso's deteriorating relationship with Olga as a negative influence on this work. Another biographical note is the sudden death of Catalan friend Ramón Pichot, who married Casegemas's lover after his tragic suicide, which had plunged Picasso into his formative Blue Period. Apparently, Pichot, the darkened character on the right of the work, would perform ancient Spanish dances which ended in a crucifix pose on the floor.

Crucifixion (1930)
Picasso Museum, Paris. Courtesy of Giraudon.
See p. 120

WOMAN IN AN ARMCHAIR (1929)

Picasso Museum, Paris. Courtesy of Giraudon

$\mathcal{G}$ROTESQUE, maniacal and lewd, this female nude is challenging in many ways. The contortion of human legs with those of the armchair, the phallic formations, the crude depiction of womb, anus and pendulous breasts are all barbaric, although it is interesting to note that their shape was briefly flirted with, more lovingly, in *The Lovers* (1919) 10 years earlier.

Often seen as related to the biomorphic style of fellow Spanish artist Joan Miró, this work is presumably a representation of the essence or protoplasm of woman as the skeletal form disintegrates, leaving a fluid, mocking sex object. For the feminist movement, the reductive invasion of face and body underlines Picasso's continual subjugation of the female image, particularly here, with the displaced vagina as mouth, complete with vicious teeth. Several commentators stress the tension in his marriage to Olga and the developing love affair with 17-year-old model Marie-Thérèse Walter as negative influences, but this was a deeply sexually charged man, approaching fifty and with all the inherent life-crises this significant age can pose.

The use of colour and patterning also mocks Matisse's work with its imitation of wallpaper design. The red and green polarisation, when juxtaposed with the calm sea outside, heightens the frenzied tension within the room.

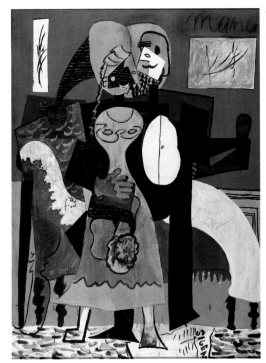

The Lovers (1919)
Musée Picasso, Paris. Courtesy of the Picasso Administration/Photo RMN–R.G. Ojeda (See p. 92)

THE CRUCIFIXION (1930)

Picasso Museum, Paris. Courtesy of Giraudon

*I*N THIS work, Picasso returns to his fascination with the 'life in death' paradox, encapsulated perfectly by the Western world's foremost symbol: the Crucifixion. The whole notion of rebirth and transformation has fascinated artists for centuries, as they see themselves as actively participating in an alchemical process while recreating life in their chosen medium.

The Crucifixion has no particular religious significance, although its interpretation of pain and suffering is intensely captured and it is a fascinating forerunner, with the use of certain shapes and expressions, to Picasso's most famous work, *Guernica* (1937). The paradoxical nature of agony, summed up in a moment called 'the Passion', is beautifully explored by his development of modern Expressionism, the movement that distorted reality to express the artist's own inner vision and emotions.

The black and white colouring is used ironically to focus on this moment of passion, which is a sensation usually associated with red, whereas paradoxically violent reds and yellows construct the surrounding scene. The juxtaposition heightens both the artistic and metaphorical paradox. The elaborate amoebic forms also create an abstract feeling, although there remains a level of pictorial representation. It is as though Picasso had reached an aesthetic crossroads and was seeking some spiritual transformation in his work.

THE ACROBAT (1930)

Musée Picasso, Paris. Courtesy of the Picasso Administration / RMN–R.G. Ojeda

*T*HE spontaneous agility of the acrobat's body is an obvious model for the new plasticity of Picasso's developing biomorphism, pioneered by fellow Spaniard Joan Miró. However, Miró rejected Cubist space and used his neo-Neolithic shapes to define new spatial concepts of freedom, often without reference to human form. In contrast, Picasso's surreal explorations maintain some human identity.

Here, despite apparent freedom of movement, this figure is still trapped within the cube of the frame. It is also bound by the colours, which strangely imprison the motion of the body, as it is locked

within a white form and then pinioned against the implied stasis of the black background. This is spatial contortion, the paradox of movement and rigidity.

One presumes the figure is male, although there is an androgyny. It is a rare interlude in a period when so many works are disfigurations of the female form. Often Surrealist works contain some sexual reference or punning, so possibly the weird, dangling phallic hand, similar to the pendulous penile limb formations of *Woman in an Armchair* (1929), is the joke. This globular phase soon died away as Picasso found a more lyrical energy by which to structure and project the human form.

Woman in an Armchair (1929)
Picasso Museum, Paris. Courtesy of Giraudon.
(See p. 119)

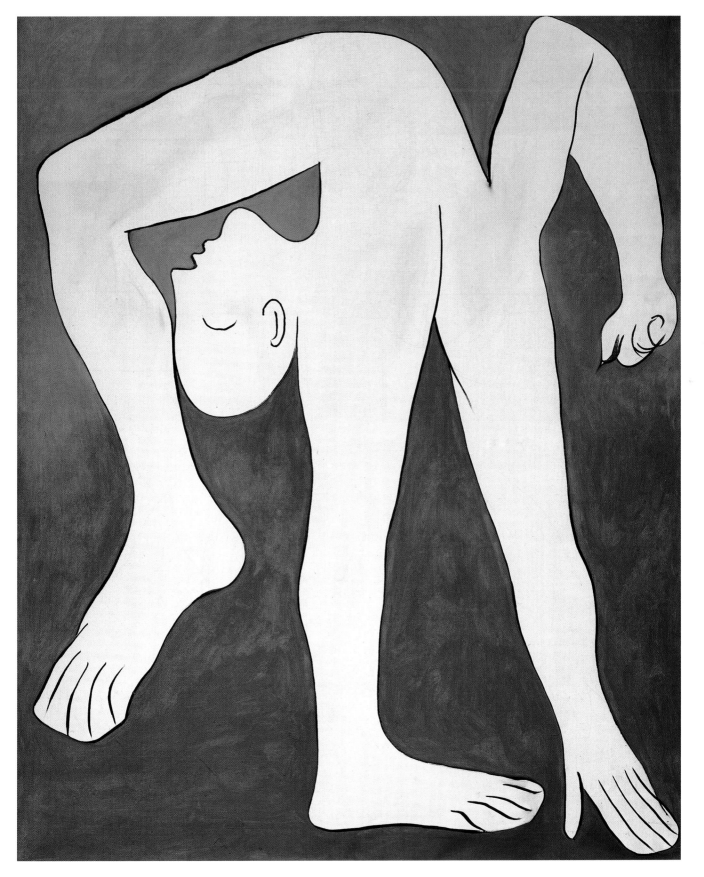

FIGURES AT THE SEASIDE (THE KISS) (1931)

Picasso Museum, Paris. Courtesy of Giraudon

A SERIES of bizarre erotic beach scenes, including *The Kiss*, was painted in the summer of 1931 at Picasso's French Riviera vacation resort, Juan-les-Pins. Said to be inspired by the 50-year-old painter's liaison with 19-year-old model, Marie-Thérèse Walter, the grotesque nature of the depicted forms reduces this moment of intimate contact to a level of crudity, probably more representative of his deteriorating relationship with his wife, Olga.

The praying mantis-like head of the two figures was a popular image with the Surrealists because the perverse concept of the female insect eating her mate after intercourse provided another visual metaphor of the 'life in death' paradox. Here, the heads incorporate Picasso's obscene *vagina dentata* teeth imagery, as well as penile tongues.

These gruesome coupled creatures appear washed ashore like sea monsters, furthering notions of primeval protoplasm, the stuff of life. It is as if Picasso is obsessed with the fundamental essence of the sexual act. Bizarrely, these metamorphic shapes are a progression of his monumental neo-Classical figuration of the early 1920s, which were also often set on the beach. Here, the perspective is drawn up close, so that the focus is firmly on the obscenely enlarged shapes.

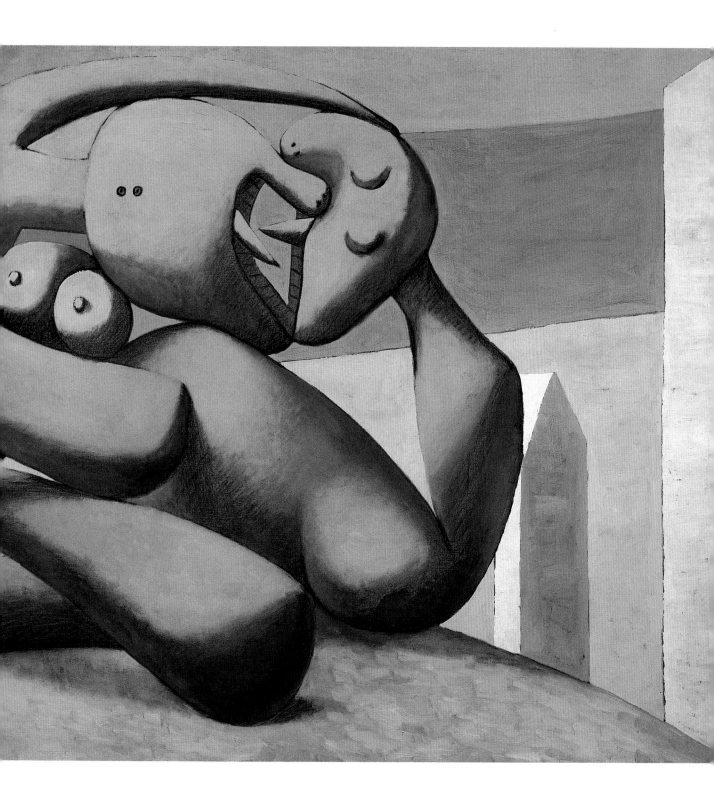

READING (1932)

Picasso Museum, Paris. Courtesy of Giraudon

Asleep (1932)
Courtesy of Christie's Images. (See p. 129)

*E*NAMOURED with Marie-Thérèse Walter, Picasso embarked on a prolific series featuring her face and profile, which progressively became more lyrical and harmonious. It marked a return to recognised signifiers of beauty as voluptuous curves and sensations of feminine sensuality began to fill the canvas once more.

The resulting lack of vulgarity is replaced by a mood of dreamy trances and self-contemplation, whether reading a book, as in this case, studying one's reflection, or resting as in *Asleep* (1932). Prototype woman now begins to be recreated into a new and much more substantial form and, like Picasso's teenager lover, embarks on an adolescent voyage of sexual and psychological awareness.

The significant development of this phase is the formalised experiment with colour, Matisse-like in choice of pigment and application. A new-found vigour bursts as colour onto the canvas as Picasso plays with Matisse's dynamic polarisation of red and green and the inclusion of patterning. The significantly heart-shape faced woman is an evolution of Synthetic Cubist productions. The closeness of her interlacing segments of colour flattens the spatial depth, despite the artist's attempt at making the picture appear three-dimensional by painting in a corner. The intensity and contrast of the wide vertical green and yellow stripes provide a tonal armature to hold the flowing lines of the female shape in place.

ASLEEP (1932)
Courtesy of Christie's Images

*A*GAIN the expansive contented mood of Picasso, once more in love, is expressed with a new artistic style. In this work, another of the Marie-Thérèse Walter series, we see her asleep, her body resting between the two powerful polarised colour blocks of red and green, whose oppositional forces accentuate her stillness. The face is denuded of expression and character, adopting the heavy mask of the gargantuan monolithic women so typical of Picasso's 1920s neo-Classical period.

The solid black outline around the girl's hands and profile is a feature of the series, recalling the Fauvist's black binding of colour blocks. The emphasised leonine hands with claw-like fingers give the figure an animalistic primitivism, which becomes a feature, as in *The Mirror* (1932), of this short style change. However, this impression of bestiality is juxtaposed by the graceful lyricism of the body's contours. It is a weird combination of beauty and ugliness, another theme that continually fascinated Picasso.

The Surrealists's dream world is intimated, but the viewer is witnessing external materiality rather than the model's subconscious mental processes. The work is more a reflection of the artist's sub-consciousness and an insight into the Andalucian concept of *mirada fuerte* – the erotic gaze – in which the voyeuristic eye becomes a sexual organ.

The Mirror (1932)
Courtesy of Christie's Images. (See p. 130)

THE MIRROR (1932)

Courtesy of Christie's Images

A NOTHER of the Marie-Thérèse Walter series, this work was followed by a sequel called *Girl Before a Mirror*, painted just two days later, in which Marie-Thérèse actually studies her mirror reflection. Later work sees her sleeping, as in *Sleeping before Green Shutters (Marie-Thérèse Walter)* (1936). Here, the fact that the mirror is blank is significant. It stresses the concept of innocence compared to the symbolic associations of comprehension, psychic revelation and the death of naivete when one regards one's image. We are waiting for the sleeping beauty to wake and pass through the centrally positioned and beckoning blank space of the mirror. Again, this work accents *mirada fuerte*, the erotic gaze of Picasso the artist, with the mirror as referent image of his absent profile.

The mirror's importance in the painting is stressed in the title and visually by the dynamic energy created by the polarised red and green curves. This gives the work a Matisse-like quality, especially with the background wallpaper study, a favourite patterning device of his. Here, Picasso's geometrics contrast subtly with the flowing body contours, creating a mesmerising rhythm of movement juxtaposed by stasis. Picasso was fascinated by Matisse's explorations of the spectrum, which usually revolved round poles of red and green to insist on the realistic flatness of the painted surface.

Sleeping before Green Shutters (Marie-Thérèse Walter) (1936)
Picasso Museum, Paris. Courtesy of Giraudon. (See p. 142)

NUDE WOMAN IN RED ARMCHAIR (1932)

Courtesy of the Tate Gallery

THE ACCENTUATION of the face with the hands signing a heart-shape is similar to earlier 1932 Marie-Thérèse work, *Reading* (1932). Again, Picasso is toying lovingly with colour, set in swirling forms, as he plays artistically with his nubile teenage lover and her voluptuousness.

However, instead of using Matisse's technique to stress the painted surface with bold colours, as in previous pictures of this sub-series, Picasso refines elements of light and shadow. The body is shaded with a pastel blue-grey, absorbed from the stronger blue of the arm and half the face. This blue is then whitened to highlight the other arm, one breast, half a face and the other hand. Consequently, the model appears to contemplate a strong light shining down, her hands framing her face coyly as she though she is transfixed, like a startled deer. Again we have a strong sensation of *mirada fuerte*, with the light source possibly signifying the erotic gaze of Picasso the artist.

Once again the polarising red and green blocks, this time on the right side of the picture, exaggerate the light source from the left, serving as a dynamic tonal armature to hold the colours and flowing forms in place.

Reading (1932)
Picasso Museum, Paris. Courtesy of Giraudon. (See p. 126)

BULLFIGHT:
DEATH OF THE TOREADOR (1933)

Picasso Museum, Paris. Courtesy of Giraudon

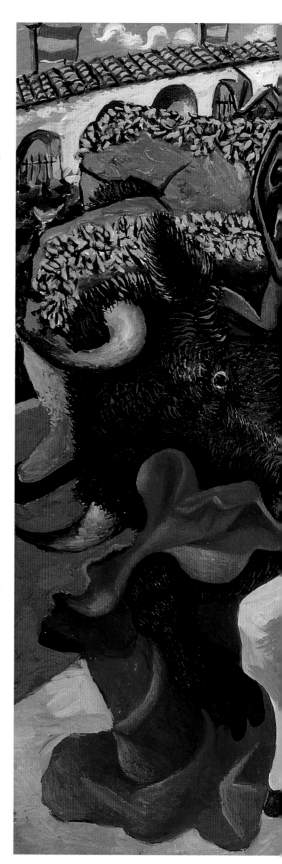

*P*ICASSO'S recent colour experiments burst onto the canvas in full technicolour glory as he returns to his favourite theme and personal passion: the bullfight. In later life he admitted that he often painted bullfights, traditionally held on Sundays, when unable to attend. This work was completed at Boisgeloup, the chateau 40 miles north-west of Paris, which Picasso, now fabulously wealthy, bought in 1930.

The central image of the panicking grey horse, with its heavy brushstrokes, acts as an imposing tonal contrast, in order to exaggerate the use of colours that capture the moment of the bullfighter's death. We hardly notice that the butchered horse is dying because the entrails are grey in tone. The absence of gore from horse and man is taken up by the referent image of the red cape, which swirls in a bloody cloud between the bull and the fighter who falls, like his cloak, between the two beasts. Colour creates a powerful sensation of crackling energy, violent movement and death.

Picasso increasingly fixates on this theme in a prophetic series, which builds towards the celebrated *Guernica* (1937), his response to the Spanish Civil War, in which this horse's head reappears. The bull's stunningly detailed profile also frequently recurs in the lead up to *Guernica*.

WOMAN IN A RED HAT (1934)

Courtesy of Topham

THE earlier curvaceous swirls that accompanied Picasso's love affair with teenager Marie-Thérèse Walter soon start to deteriorate, as can be seen in this work. A new phase, returning to the angularity and distortion associated with Cubism, is being redefined but within the invigorated colour framework developed during the Marie-Thérèse sub-series.

To moderate this renewed sharpness, Picasso includes organic forms that sprout colourfully out of the black ground; a plant on the table and by the chair leg, and a sunflower behind.

The exaggerated, angular nose seems to be a development of the close-up profile of the face from his earlier work, *Asleep* (1932). But the face, with its distorted eyes, and the body both have a sense of fantasy, allying the work to Surrealism. The odd white shape of the leg, an extension of the model's clothing, blends into shoes, although it shares much in common with a chair or table leg.

The form is disquieting and challenging as it straddles the perspective of a corner, defined by the black and white background. This contrast creates spatial depth so that the woman is set back from the picture surface. The general distortion again dissembles common aesthetic notions of beauty, forcing the viewers to challenge their own concepts.

Asleep (1932)
Courtesy of Christie's Images. (See p. 129)

MINOTAUROMACHY (1935)

Picasso Museum, Paris. Courtesy of AiSA

*T*HIS stunning etching is a portentous milestone in Picasso's career as the themes of bullfighting and the mythological Minotaur are symbolically examined in metaphysical and political terms. *Minotauromachy* is always critically recognised as a major forerunner to *Guernica* (1937).

Like other works of this period, the Minotaur is transformed to bestial man with a predatory, Bacchanalian devouring of nubile girls. Whether symbolic of Picasso's own sexual potency, masculine ascendancy, or of evil overpowering innocence, this aggressive motif assumes varying roles and creates a web of sub-texts; making it unsurprising that many psychoanalysts have agitated over its implications.

Here, purity and innocence calmly win over aggression and adversity. The small, neatly dressed girl, in the bullring, holds up a symbolic protective candle, the image of the spiritual light of life from religious paintings, its light reaching out expressively in a halo. Around her are death, chaos and destruction. The Minotaur, with its muscular male torso and horrific, super-enlarged animal head, is an echo of *Bullfight: Death of the Toreador* (1933). Here, the disembowelled horse is bearing a dying female matador. As a frightened man escapes up the ladder, the girl remains serenely fearless and smiling. The reductionist use of black and white, light and shadow, wonderfully enhances aesthetic and philosophical concepts of simplicity, purity and truth.

Death of the Toreador (1933)
Picasso Museum, Paris. Courtesy of Giraudon. (See p. 134)

THE MUSE (1935)

Gallery of Modern Art, Paris. Courtesy of Topham

THE Marie-Thérèse Walter series, now retreating into renewed dislocation and angularity, features the model in active occupation rather than asleep or in trance-like self-reflection. *The Muse* is a fascinating picture because it features two women, one dressed and asleep, the other nude but awake, and drawing her own reflection in the mirror. It is possible that both figures are manifestations of the same woman – who, when asleep, is paradoxically liberated into action in another world – a recurrent Surrealist motif.

Picasso's favourite theme, 'life in death' is also in operation here on many levels. The female painter is actively recreating herself as a portrait, which invokes the Romantic paradox of *doppelganger* – namely that one dies on seeing one's double. More interesting is that Marie-Thérèse, Picasso's muse, lover and picture subject, is controversially pregnant at this time. In pregnancy, the muse becomes creator like her artist master, and ironically by her master, so Picasso enigmatically and egotistically portrays her at his occupation.

The reflection in the mirror is more revealing. Possibly of another work, its squiggly outline recalls mother and child images of Picasso's first lover-muse, Madeleine, who had aborted his baby exactly 30 years ago in 1905; another 'life in death' twist whose painful irony would not have been lost on Picasso.

SLEEPING BEFORE GREEN SHUTTERS (MARIE-THÉRÈSE WALTER) (1936)

Picasso Museum, Paris. Courtesy of Giraudon

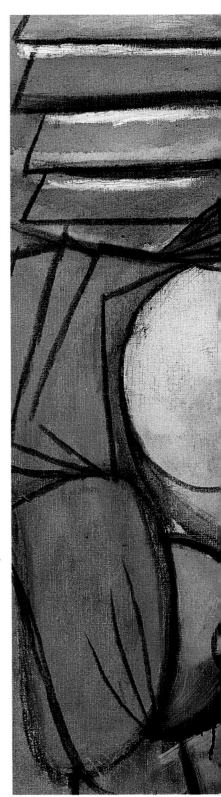

ERE Picasso is contemplating the helpless, innocent sleep of muse, lover and young mother to his new child, daughter, Maïa, named after Picasso's beloved sister who died as a child. Consequently the weird 'life in death' sub-text continues apace as Picasso makes a sentimental artistic pilgrimage to his early days of the Blue Period, recalled, as discussed in the last work, by Marie-Thérèse's pregnancy. His daughter's birth stirred up past memories of a sister who had died 30 years before.

Although executed in oil on canvas, this work has strong watercolour qualities, as the thin blue and green colours fade together, and the shutters' downward dripping paint emphasises the notion of closure. The eyes are like the heavy shutters, one signifying the other. The ring-like circles of the eyes are reiterated in the earring and in the bulbous, lactating, heavy breasts. Recalling the pain of grief as a young man, which was commemorated in the Blue Period, he re-adopts its subterranean colours, which are often associated symbolically with the sub-conscious and sadness.

During this time the couple secretly escaped with Maïa to Juan-les-Pins in the south of France; fleeing from Olga and Picasso's ugly divorce proceedings. These were eventually dropped because of complicated property laws. The artist was registered as Maïa's 'godfather' but dotingly played the role of father.

SEATED WOMAN (MARIE-THÉRÈSE WALTER) (1937)

Picasso Museum, Paris. Courtesy of Giraudon

*T*HIS joyful work was painted at the start of an amazingly prolific year, in which Picasso produced many powerful creations, including *Guernica* (1937). The influence of his young love and muse had recharged him, and he became a legend in his own lifetime. This painting has a sense of harlequinade, as strong bright bands of colour are arranged so that the dress appears like a costume. The figure may also resemble a queen court card from a deck of playing cards, whose imagery is often designed with stripes and banding creatively reversed on the same plane. Here, the bands of colour are superbly controlled by the black or white striations to create a wonderful series of energetic patterns across the contours of the body.

Picasso again returns to his technique of red and green polarisation to add a further dimension of animation. This colour combination usually creates a flatness of the picture surface but he mitigates this beautifully with the construction of a Cubist sense of spatial depth. This is created by the illusion of the two corners in the tightly receding room behind the figure. As a result, the powerful body of Marie-Thérèse, whose face recalls *Woman in a Red Hat* (1934), projects from the picture in sharp relief.

Woman in a Red Hat (1934)
Courtesy of Topham. (See p. 136)

SEATED WOMAN (MARIE-THÉRÈSE WALTER) (1937)

Picasso Museum, Paris. Courtesy of Giraudon

*T*HIS joyful work was painted at the start of an amazingly prolific year, in which Picasso produced many powerful creations, including *Guernica* (1937). The influence of his young love and muse had recharged him, and he became a legend in his own lifetime. This painting has a sense of harlequinade, as strong bright bands of colour are arranged so that the dress appears like a costume. The figure may also resemble a queen court card from a deck of playing cards, whose imagery is often designed with stripes and banding creatively reversed on the same plane. Here, the bands of colour are superbly controlled by the black or white striations to create a wonderful series of energetic patterns across the contours of the body.

Picasso again returns to his technique of red and green polarisation to add a further dimension of animation. This colour combination usually creates a flatness of the picture surface but he mitigates this beautifully with the construction of a Cubist sense of spatial depth. This is created by the illusion of the two corners in the tightly receding room behind the figure. As a result, the powerful body of Marie-Thérèse, whose face recalls *Woman in a Red Hat* (1934), projects from the picture in sharp relief.

Woman in a Red Hat (1934)
Courtesy of Topham. (See p. 136)

PORTRAIT OF DORA MAAR (1937)

Picasso Museum, Paris. Courtesy of Giraudon

*P*ICASSO painted a series of Dora Maar images over the ensuing few years as her influence gained a hold on both his political and creative life. Daughter of a Yugoslav architect, painter and photographer, Dora was originally invited by Picasso to photograph his studio. They became close friends, especially as she spoke fluent Spanish, having lived in Argentina with her family. Eventually they became lovers, and subsequently collaborators, as Picasso experimented in new photographic techniques with her.

In early 1937, Dora helped him choose a new studio in Paris and was actively involved in the creation of *Guernica* that same year, which she photographed at various development stages as an historic record.

Unlike the images of Marie-Thérèse, such as in *Woman with a Beret* (1938), Maar's obvious intellectual superiority and ability to engage Picasso as an equal is somehow conveyed in this work. The face has a strong sense of intelligence, with the eyes looking knowingly down at the viewer and the hand thoughtfully framing the face, as if in a moment of great discernment. The use of yellow as facial pigmentation adds to the aura of intelligent brightness, and the red lips and nails emphasise her cosmetic, cultured sophistication.

Woman with a Beret (1938)
Courtesy of Christie's Images. (See p. 156)

GUERNICA (1937)

The Prado, Madrid. Courtesy of Giraudon

*P*ROBABLY Picasso's most famous work, *Guernica* is certainly
his most powerful political statement, painted as an immediate
reaction to the Nazis' devastating casual bombing practice on
the Basque town of Guernica during the Spanish Civil War. A
monumental 26-foot mural, *Guernica* was art's condemnation of
Fascism as represented by General Franco and the rise of Hitler. It
pre-figured the world's horror. Here, the destructive energy of hatred
and war explodes like a bomb as appaling images of mutilation, death
and destruction, explored in the earlier bull paintings, reach an
anguished crescendo. Apocalyptic of the Second World War and nuclear

age, Picasso's iconography becomes a profound statement upon the horror and futility of war in twentieth century.

The work is seen as an amalgamation of pastoral and epic styles. Like *The Crucifixion* (1930), it relies on a central pyramidal structure and the balance between curves and straight lines. The discarding of colour intensifies the drama, producing a reportage quality as if in a photographic record.

Picasso had already been invited to paint a mural for the Paris World Fair's Spanish pavilion before the bombing happened. Starting in May 1937, *Guernica* was installed by mid June. Realising that his work would be a controversial statement, Picasso allowed Dora Maar to photograph its rapid execution for historical purposes.

WORKING DRAWING FOR GUERNICA (1937)
The Prado, Madrid. Courtesy of AiSA

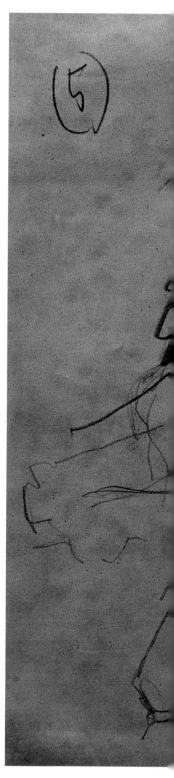

WORKING from newspaper accounts of the bombing of Guernica, Picasso drew 50 studies, subsuming motifs such as this horse, which was eventually centred dramatically in the final painting, although with its head facing the other way.

Like other works, there is a massive overlaying of significance within the allegorical sub-text. Picasso plundered his own private symbolic world of meanings to express his horror at the bombing. This screaming horse is featured in *Bullfight: Death of the Toreador* (1933), with its mighty, up-stretched neck and crumpled body powerfully expressing its final death-throes. One can almost hear the screams, the crushing of bodies, the tearing of limbs. It is a vivid onslaught on the viewers' emotions.

Some critics warn against trusting the political message in *Guernica*: for instance the rampaging bull, a major motif of destruction here, has previously figured, whether as a bull or Minotaur, as Picasso's ego. In *Guernica*, its phallic tongue can imply sexual union but is also linked with the death of a child in the arms of its mother. Perhaps Picasso was again recalling painful deaths from his own past. However, in this instance the bull probably represents the onslaught of Fascism. Picasso said it meant brutality and darkness, presumably reminiscent of his

prophetic *Minotauromachy*. He also stated that the horse represented the people of Guernica.

Guernica (1937)
The Prado, Madrid.
Courtesy of Giraudon
(See p. 148)

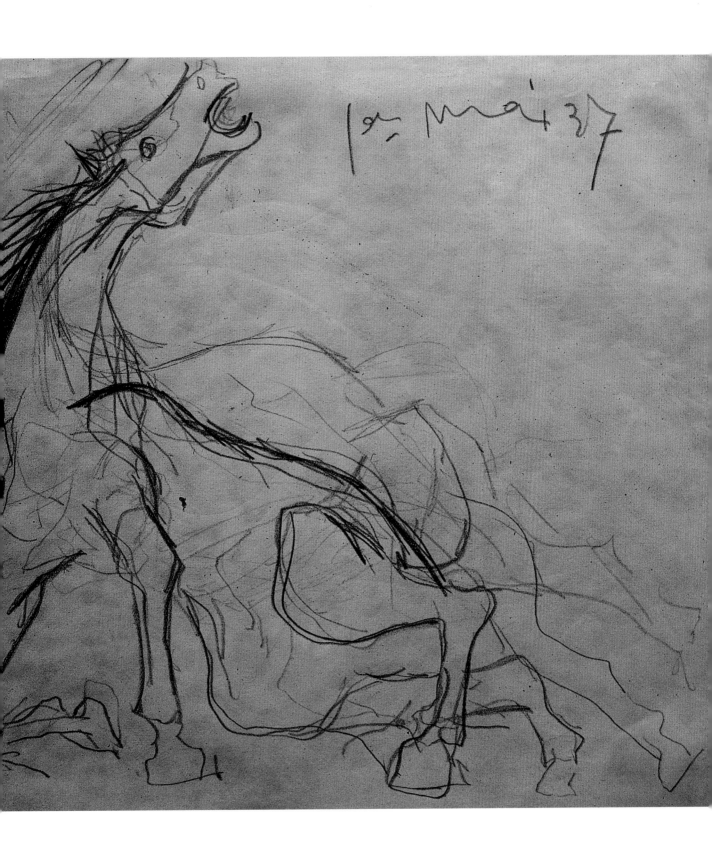

THE BEACH, JUAN-LES-PINS (1937)

Courtesy of Christie's Images

*I*N THE aftermath of the Guernica work, Picasso once again returns to the stillness of a landscape scene, as if taking breath from emotional onslaught. This mood of artistic escapism was used before, as in *Gósol* (1906), when he rediscovered freedom in the Spanish Alps following his impoverished time in Paris.

Commentators often reflect that this beach scene of *Juan-les-Pins*, dated 13th August, represents Picasso's evident exhilaration and triumph following the production of his masterpiece *Guernica* (1937). However, this work, unlike anything produced before, is also laden with political comment. The prominent French flag, centred in the composition, is significantly flying freely over this brightly coloured world of a happy and relaxed *beau monde*. The flag's three colours, which represent liberty, equality and fraternity, are echoed in the surrounding scene of striped beach huts and fishing boats.

This is a safe and bountiful haven, and Picasso is no doubt reflecting on the absurdity of the world; that while people are dying in a civil war over the border in neighbouring Spain, France is still at peace, amusing itself in the sun and enjoying the pleasures of life. It was certainly Picasso's artistic and emotional sanctuary at the time.

WEEPING WOMAN (1937)
Courtesy of the Tate Gallery

*T*HIS work is often viewed as a post-script picture to *Guernica* (1937), due to the concepts of agony and distress that are further explored within it. Painted the day after Picasso's 56th birthday, the depictions of grief are interesting as one can question the model's identity: both Marie-Thérèse and Dora Maar featured prominently in his life at the time.

The dark hair, with the lighter striations to define movement, is similar to depictions of Dora in an earlier work the same year, *Portrait of Dora Maar*, though blond Marie-Thérèse had also modelled for works in which the female figure had black, green and even blue hair.

The distinctive over-dramatised eyes, with heavy eye lashing and brows, now become a feature of Picasso's work, as do the new facial deformations. The breaking up of recognised facial characteristics continues apace as angular shapes and mask-like sectioning, reminiscent of *Les Demoiselles d'Avignon* (1907) and the ensuing Cubist era, return in a more sophisticated and complex format. The tortured, jagged patterning sharpens the inferences of pain and sorrow, especially the whitened-out area around the mouth, which creates a skull-like, death-mask appearance. It is as if the skin is peeled back to reveal the physical mechanics of grief. The manic-like distortions also make the work cartoonesque.

Portrait of Dora Maar (1937)
Picasso Museum, Paris. Courtesy of Giraudon. (See p. 146)

WOMAN WITH A BERET (1938)

Courtesy of Christie's Images

PAINTED at the start of the new year, this picture marks a richness of invention that gained momentum as Picasso was filled with creative vigour and enthusiasm from his success with *Guernica* the previous year. Here, the facial structure, hair and expression are similar to that of his daughter Maïa in *Maïa with a Doll*, executed shortly after this portrait. The later picture helps to identify the model as Maïa's mother Marie-Thérèse Walter, Picasso's young mistress, who is often shown wearing a hat.

There is a continuing strong plasticity of form, even though many of the facial characteristics seem angular, such as the prominent nose and slanting eye definitions. These oppositional tensions play dynamically in many of the female figures at this time, as the pliable form is continually folded and stretched in inquiry.

Again, red and green are polarised to provide a further dynamic energy to the work. However, the gradual muting of the background into hints of yellow and orange, taken from the beret, serve to accentuate the significance of the hat. Defined by a loose grid of red lines, the remaining form is produced by the yellow pigment, making the hat shimmer beautifully like a golden crown as it sits between the red and green polarisation.

Maïa with a Doll (1938)
Picasso Museum, Paris.
Courtesy of Giraudon. (See p. 159)

MAÏA WITH A DOLL (1938)

Picasso Museum, Paris. Courtesy of Giraudon

Paulo Picasso as Harlequin (1924)
Picasso Museum, Paris. Courtesy of Giraudon.
(See p. 114)

*A*S DAUGHTER Maïa plays with her doll, adoring father Picasso plays with his latest artistic processing of space and colour. The recent plastic phase of figurative distortion is continued, while the characteristics of the face are pushed and remoulded, as though constructed from modelling clay. As always, Picasso's sense of fun and humour surface: the doll has the real face, whereas that of the child is surreal, a beautiful juxtaposition. Both heads are absurdly enlarged compared to the rest of the body. The doll's eyes match Maïa's outfit and Maïa's match the doll's sailor's costume, and so the child is interchangeable with the doll.

The doll is probably a bizarre signifier for Picasso the father, who as a child was also pictured dressed in such an outfit. In the same way, Picasso was interchangeable with his son Paulo in the harlequin costume in his portrait of 1924. Despite the modernist distortions, this painting of Maïa is suggestive of that earlier sentimental picture. The cuffs, ruffs and frills of sixteenth-century Spanish master Velázquez, featured in the Paulo portrait, return here in Maïa's frothy attire. They serve to define the body's pyramidal outline against the simplistic horizontal blocks of brown and white that separate the floor and wall planes.

STILL LIFE, FRUIT AND WATER JUG (1939)
Courtesy of Christie's Images

*T*HIS wonderful still life is so full of the vitality, vigour and sense of humour that became characteristic of the pre-war part of Picasso's work this year. It is a far call from the geometric still-life Cubist days and is an interesting development of the looser, freer form Picasso was working with.

Once again, the style owes a debt to Matisse, who, significantly, was to exhibit with Picasso in Boston, USA, later in 1939. Picasso plays, like his rival, with a challenging, lyrical rhythm in which a swirling form is balanced by the interplay of colours. As Picasso once said, 'Matisse alone tickled painting into such bursts of laughter.'

The exploration of the relationship between the apple and pitcher became a persistent mini-series as an amusing interlude to the almost obsessive drawing of the women in his life during these years, and this work is probably one of the series' stronger executions. The blues and greens provide an interesting aura of tonal contrast, effectively used in *Sleeping before Green Shutters (Marie-Thérèse Walter)* (1936), but here held together by the shared secondary colour, yellow, used as the base to link the two objects together. The flowing black shadowing adds further impressions of spatial depth, as well as rhythm to the work.

Sleeping before Green Shutters (Marie-Thérèse Walter) (1936)
Picasso Museum, Paris. Courtesy of Giraudon. (See p. 142)

WOMEN AT THEIR TOILET (1938)

Picasso Museum, Paris. Courtesy of Giraudon

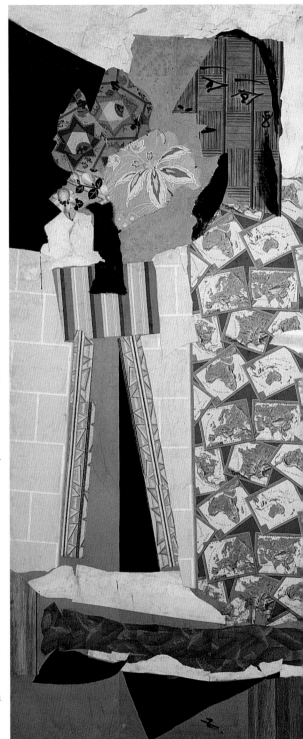

THIS wonderful post-Cubist work is a massive collation of Synthetic Cubist papiers-collés techniques, alongside elements of Picasso's current plasticity of the female form. Measuring a mammoth 3 x 4.5 m (10 x 14.5 ft), the work is a combination of oil and huge strips of pasted wallpaper on canvas. Several artistic devices have been incorporated from Picasso's earlier exploratory work with Georges Braque, such as the overlays of wallpaper, decorative mouldings and other interior design representations.

The women's eyes and facial shapes are all comparable with other Picasso works of the time, but the malleability of form is lost. These women sit on the canvas like one-dimensional, cut-out paper dolls. As one woman combs the centrally seated figure's hair, another holds up a mirror to watch the toilet – the reflected face is a fantastical swirling image in blue.

Executed in the spring of 1938, the work is also known as *Cartoon for a Tapestry*. No doubt Picasso is punning on both artistic meanings for 'cartoon', recalling the traditional Old Masters' term for a full-scale, detailed preparatory drawing or painting as well as the modern meaning for a satirical drawing.

SEATED WOMAN (1938)

Norman Granz Private Collection. Courtesy of Topham

T HE revisiting of Synthetic Cubist techniques in *Women At Their Toilet* (1938) commences the collapse of Picasso's recent explorations of the plastic form into a more rigid phase. Suddenly, the flowing forms are filled with an intricate network of web-like lines that interconnect shapes and colour, creating alternative rhythmic patterns and tensions.

Initial workings leading up to this picture show how Picasso played with the human form, using a series of basketwork-style lines to create a skeletal shape. These basketwork constructions developed during 1938 into this involved configuration of colours and lines.

Considering Picasso's earlier works this decade, such as *Reading* (1932), one can see how his work progressed logically in this direction.

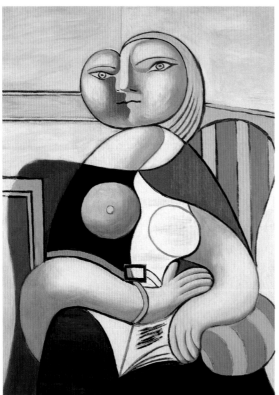

Again, the viewer sees the skull-like facial development from other recent works, but the recent apple-shaped, fecund breasts now have a life of their own. In fact, the study is simply electric as the energy pours out of the canvas in all directions, though the violence of this energy is possibly moderated by the choice of a pastel palette, which was unusual for Picasso.

The work was painted in Mougins, in the south of France, which was Picasso's favourite haunt with his other mistress, Dora Maar, with whom he spent the summer.

Reading (1932)
Picasso Museum, Paris. Courtesy of Giraudon.
(See p. 126)

RECLINING WOMAN WITH A BOOK (MARIE-THÉRÈSE WALTER) (1939)

Picasso Museum, Paris. Courtesy of Giraudon

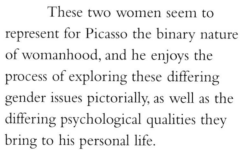

*P*ICASSO'S notions of Marie-Thérèse Walter's innocent beauty continued to drive him, with this return to the voluptuous lines that had inspired this decade's gradual development of plasticity of form. This work is one of a pair, actually painted on the same day, of both of the women in his life in the same pose, but exploring a different morphology. The picture of the sharp and intelligent Dora Maar is hard and angular, as in the recent basketwork compositions, with intimations of fecundity suggested by the inclusion of organic forms seen through the background window. Marie-Thérèse, as shown here, is contrastingly soft and feminine; with her ample curves and round face, she was Picasso's concept of the perfect earth mother.

These two women seem to represent for Picasso the binary nature of womanhood, and he enjoys the process of exploring these differing gender issues pictorially, as well as the differing psychological qualities they bring to his personal life.

The colour polarisation is similar to earlier representations of Marie-Thérèse, such as *Nude Woman on a Red Armchair* (1932). However, here the red and green polarisation creates a strong, diagonal tension across the canvas so that as the gentler blue form rests within this energy force field, an aura of relaxation is emphasised.

Nude Woman in Red Armchair (1932)
Courtesy of the Tate Gallery. *(See p. 132)*

STILL LIFE, FRUIT DISH WITH FRUIT AND VASE WITH FLOWERS (1939)

Courtesy of Christie's Images

DESPITE the death of Picasso's mother at the start of the year, followed by the invasion of Barcelona and Madrid by Franco's forces and the annexing of Prague by Hitler, this picture from the early summer gives the impression that life was good for Picasso. In fact, it was like a bowl of cherries.

Picasso explores a romantic timbre as colours leap from the canvas and the china images adopt a loose lyrical form, defined and held in place by the blue lines of the china's patterning. The profusion of colour from the cherries is almost Pointillist, as layers of varying shades of red pigment are exquisitely dotted on the canvas. It is simplistic but cheery as bright objects crowd the canvas and fill the space with their offerings.

Again, a Matisse-like strong patterning device, the green–blue checked tablecloth, is employed to counterbalance the rhythmic motion of the forms. This checking adds a sense of grounding to the overall composition, even though its perspective is incongruous; one is not sure where the table ends.

The depiction of china is interesting. Picasso had not yet properly explored the world of ceramics, although he became increasingly fascinated with it after the Second World War and this interest lasted into his extreme old age.

CAT AND BIRD (1939)

Picasso Museum, Paris. Courtesy of Giraudon

THE sombre and sinister mood of this dark work pre-empts the splendid masterpiece of *Night Fishing at Antibes* (1939). This depiction of the final death throes of the helpless bird is predatory, and suggests a malignant stealth instead of the rampaging savagery of *Guernica* (1937). However, it is still a powerful and celebrated oeuvre, with the cat's accentuated silvered claws, the gruesome teeth and odd black and white forms for eyes.

The colours here are more simplistic than *Night Fishing at Antibes*, yet they still achieve powerful results. The pale lilac-blue background, representative of the night, heightens the dark, mangy form of the tabby cat as well as the bird's stark shape. The silver white contouring of the cat's back legs and one front leg adds a frisson of energy and tension, highlighting the cat's power and ability to pounce.

Painted in the spring of 1939, there is a profound message in this work. The cat becomes more symbolic when one considers that politically, Europe was crumbling under the stealthy and predatory nature of Fascism. Picasso was sickened by Franco's final invasion of Barcelona in January 1939, the fall of Madrid just before this was completed, and the annexing of Prague by Hitler.

Night Fishing at Antibes (1939)
The Museum of Modern Art, New York. Mrs Simon Guggenheim Fund. Courtesy of the Museum of Modern Art, New York. (See p. 172)

NIGHT FISHING AT ANTIBES (1939)

Mrs Simon Guggenheim Fund. Courtesy of The Museum of Modern Art, New York

*A*S THE gloom and fear of another world war loomed, Picasso captured Europe's black mood stunningly in this haunting nocturne. It is another massive work, at 205 x 345 cm (7 x 11 ft), which, like *Guernica* (1937), is sub-divided into large triangular groupings.

Picasso spent the summer of 1939 on the French Riviera with Dora Maar and his regular entourage. Inspiration for this picture came during evening walks with Dora, when they watched the fishermen at work underneath their night-lights to attract the fish. She can be seen on the right-hand jetty, holding her bicycle and eating an ice cream.

The huge central fisherman figure, with his Neptune-like trident-spear, takes on mythological proportions. His simplistic form and expression are at odds with any notion of godhead, but in this world the simple man is empowered as king. As in *The Beach, Juan-les-Pins* (1937), executed at the start of the Spanish Civil War, Picasso is fascinated that basic life still goes on in spite of world events.

Although the forms might be simple, the use of colour, like the political backdrop, is complex. The work has a powerful, cavernous, subterranean quality as shades of violet, green, yellow and red emerge from, and then fade back into the darkness.

WOMAN READING (1939)

Courtesy of Christie's Images

*P*ICASSO left Paris for Royan on the French Atlantic coast when Germany invaded Poland on 1st September 1939. He stayed in a hotel with Dora, keeping Marie-Thérèse and Maïa in a nearby villa. The town, near Bordeaux, was for the time being safe and far enough away from Paris.

Picasso always stated that he never directly painted the Second World War, but nevertheless agreed that it did influence his work. Historians would later demonstrate how it had transformed his style. Already a darkened, bloody tone can be felt creeping into the intensity of the deep red of this sombre work.

The series of 1930s reading pictures usually featured Marie-Thérèse, and she was probably the model for this work. The cartoonesque feet recall an earlier work, *Woman in a Red Hat* (1934), in shape and design. However, the most striking feature of this work is the heavy white outlining around the blackened upper torso. This recalls the silvery-white lining on the cat in a similarly powerful work, *Cat and Bird* (1939), which connoted the movement of pouncing. Here, the large, heavy, scratched-in white striations make the figure leap out of the canvas in a ghostly format, exuding, in this moment of stillness while reading, some spiritual presence.

Cat and Bird (1939)
Picasso Museum, Paris. Courtesy of Giraudon. (See p.170)

PORTRAIT OF SABARTÉS (1939)
The Sabartés Collection. Courtesy of AiSA

*T*HIS humorous portrait of Picasso's life-long Spanish friend, secretary and chief legend-monger is a wonderful joke. In 1938, Jaime Sabartés asked Picasso to draw him as a sixteenth-century royal courtier; those original drawings were eventually turned into this oil, painted at Royan. Portraying Sabartés as a Spanish courtier to Philip II is amusing as this was the role he played in the court of Picasso; that of the loyal servant following his master from Paris to Antibes to Royan. Although Sabartés was often represented by critics as a pathetically faithful dog, Picasso no doubt respected and returned his loyalty – albeit in his own fashion.

In comparison with the Sabartés portrait from 1901, one can see how far Picasso has progressed from his early days, when as young men they explored the bohemian Parisian café life of Montmartre. Here, the return to the recent plastic deformations of the face only serves to accentuate the ludicrous nature of the portrait and its notions of masquerade. But within the work, joker Picasso is also playing at masquerade, parodying the grand Spanish art master El Greco, who painted the Spanish courtiers of Philip II, and who was admired, like Picasso, for his revolutionary contortions.

Sabartés (Le Bock or Glass of Beer) (1901)
Pushkin Museum, Moscow. Courtesy of Art Resource. (See p. 22)

PORTRAIT OF DORA MAAR (1941)

Courtesy of Christie's Images

DORA Maar still continued to be an abiding creative and intellectual influence in Picasso's life, particularly during the early war years. Here, instead of exploring her form in oil Picasso returned to the papiers-collés days of Synthetic Cubism with this highly effective, small, square-shaped work. The dress is fashioned out of folded wallpaper and the face is drawn using gouache, with a golden leaf collage to crown her as his muse. This is mounted on corrugated board whose horizontal lines add an extra dimensional pattern and effective contrast with the chequering of the dress.

The board's colour is also echoed in the skin tones, which are a striking grey-blue wash, taking the colour from the dress. Despite the chilling effect of this employment of colour, there is a strong sense of harmony and balance about the work. Unlike Picasso's recent return to plastic distortion, the depiction is almost naturalistic. Its proportions make the head just a little larger than life-size, so to a viewer it would be like confronting Dora face-on. However, unlike the portrait of 1937, the startling eyes look out to the horizon rather than down at the viewer. The long aquiline nose still suggests a distanced haughtiness.

Portrait of Dora Maar (1937)
Picasso Museum, Paris.
Courtesy of Giraudon. (See p. 146)

WOMAN SITTING IN AN ARMCHAIR (1941)
Courtesy of Christie's Images

*A*S THE war gained momentum, Picasso increasingly returned to a flat, two-dimensional style, with his figures close to the canvas surface, as in this work. Figural dislocation and distortion seem most acute as the angularity is intensified. There are several armchair pictures of the time, though this particular version sees a repeat of the chair from *Woman Reading* (1939).

Earlier works of 1941 were more subdued in colour, but even though this one features a stronger palette, there is still a loss of gaiety and brilliance. When the Germans captured France, Picasso returned to Paris and moved into his studio, installing Marie-Thérèse and Maïa in a nearby apartment. Despite pleas from friends to escape to the USA or Mexico, the artist believed his fame gave him immunity, despite the fact that many of his acquaintances were arrested. Tragically, the Jewish poet and Picasso's friend, Max Jacob, died of pneumonia in a concentration camp.

French soldiers occupied Picasso's chateau of Boisgeloup, destroying plaster sculptures in the studio. There were shortages everywhere and art materials were difficult to obtain. At the start of the year, Picasso wrote a farce, poking fun at the spartan conditions, in which the characters were obsessed by cold, hunger and love. However his determination and his resolute presence in Paris eventually made him a prominent symbol for the French Resistance.

Woman Reading (1939)
Courtesy of Christie's Images. (See p. 174)

WOMAN WITH DARK EYES (1941)
Courtesy of SKM/Per Anders Allsten

THIS portrait is presumably another image of Dora Maar, as the facial qualities are very similar to *Portrait of Dora Maar* (1941), even though there is a change of headgear. Maar was renown for her extravagant clothes and hats, though the pleated aspect of this head-piece, which is echoed in the distortion of the top of her arm, becomes an interesting structural device in later works where it develops into a basketwork technique for exploring form.

Dora's light grey-blue wash face in the earlier portrait has now progressed tonally to include a greeny turquoise and a slight polarising reddy-orange hue around the nose. Again this serves to create an impression of distanced haughtiness about the sitter, setting her face back from the surface of the canvas. The use of turquoise here to create a sensation of distance and separation is employed to greater effect in Picasso's final years, in works such as *Landscape* (1967) and *Seated Woman with a Hat* (1971). The large dramatic eyes, subject of the picture's title, and exaggerated by the use of heavy black rimming, also become a significant feature of Picasso's later portraits of his second wife, Jacqueline Roque.

Portrait of Dora Maar (1941)
Courtesy of Christie's Images. (See p. 179)

STILL LIFE WITH STEER'S SKULL (1942)

Dusseldorf Kunstsammlung. Courtesy of Topham

During the build up to and during the war, Picasso often played directly with the theme of death in a series of still-lifes depicting animal skulls. Usually, these skulls were sheep's heads rather than, as portrayed here, a steer, (a young castrated bullock). The implied death of the young bull is obviously an interesting choice of motif from the Picasso repertoire of this time. It suggests notions of impotence – artistic restriction, as well as Fascism – following the bull's appearance in *Guernica* (1937). Perhaps this work is Picasso's pictorial death wish for the Fascists.

Still Life with Steer's Skull echoes the colouring of the picture painted on the eve of the Second World War: *Night Fishing at Antibes* (1939), but the intensity of the hideous whitened skull against the sombre funereal colours is also reminiscent of dramatisation techniques used in *Cat and Bird* and *Woman Reading*, both of 1939. Later works are lighter, such as *Glass and Fruit* (1944), but here the skull appears to lift off the canvas, giving its dead form a notion of animation. The exposure of the front bottom teeth recalls the gnashing jaws of the pitiful dying horse in *Guernica*. Yet, unlike *Guernica*'s study of explosive movement, which captures the imagery of war, this registers stasis and the psychological restrictions associated with enemy occupation.

Glass and Fruit (1944)
Courtesy of Christie's Images.
(See p. 190)

THE ROOSTER (1943)

Courtesy of Christie's Images

I N 1938, Picasso introduced cockerel imagery into his work, exploring the bird's movements and facial contortions. This return to the theme in 1943 sees a more reductionist approach to the subject matter. Here, the bird's body appears clipped and tight, though the motion of flapping wings, featured explicitly in earlier works, is depicted by the orange and red fan shape that energetically breaks free from the restrained background. The exaggerated circular motion of the tail feathers also creates a sense of movement, in contrast to the tight, angular pyramidal structure of the body.

The work conveys a sense of the helplessness of war, as in the more predatory picture, *Cat and Bird* (1939). But like the bird in the earlier work, the squawking of this pathetic angry creature is futile – its noise is insignificant against the backdrop of the night.

Cat and Bird (1939)
Picasso Museum, Paris. Courtesy of Giraudon. (See p. 170)

However, the bird could have another significance and symbolise America, which, at this time, had finally entered the war. Apparently when first asked why he painted the rooster series, Picasso replied, 'there have always been cocks, but like everything else in life we must discover them – cocks have always been seen but never as well as in American weather vanes.'

THE BLUE COFFEE POT (1944)

Courtesy of Christie's Images

THIS work, painted in the spring of 1944, is like the return of an old friend, recollecting the later days of Cubism. There is an angular cutting of shapes and shadows as the spatial form is explored. The pot's long body is stretched up the surface and is further exaggerated by the length of the canvas: 61 cm (almost 2 ft) in length. Yet Picasso creates a sense of depth with the three-dimensional effect of the pot and the regressive plane of the table.

The tripartite colours and their hues are reminiscent of *Woman Reading* (1939) though the red, white and blue could also signify of the French national flag and its meanings of freedom, equality and fraternity. If so, it is a subtle inclusion.

By 1944, many of Picasso's friends had fled, been arrested or died in German captivity. Jealous collaborationists, such as the artist Vlaminck, attempted to denounce Picasso falsely to the authorities as a Jew or psychotic. Although he kept a low political profile, Picasso was in regular contact with the French Resistance, which met over coffee in bars and bistros around Paris. After the war he was invited to do the first drawing for a commemorative book to be given to General de Gaulle from Resistance writers and artists.

Woman Reading (1939)
Courtesy of Christie's Images. (See p. 174)

GLASS AND FRUIT (1944)

Courtesy of Christie's Images

RARELY published, this work is remarkable in that it signposts Picasso's next development – of simplistic child-like forms and freer use of colour. Although a small oil on canvas – just 22 x 27 cm (8.5 x 10.5 ins) – its simplicity is stunning. Painted just ten days after the D-day landings and the final assault of the Allies into France, the work has a bright note of optimism, even though the last days of the war saw regular street shootings and increased tension in Paris.

The still life is a loose collection of simple forms, linked again by the network grid of a tablecloth. It is a reductionist study of geometric forms with the round fruit, possibly cherries, a square yellow box, maybe a napkin, and the simplistic form of a cylinder to represent the glass. These objects are held in place by a heavily defined, thickly painted black outline. The brightness of the primary colours is concentrated, especially the bold yellow square, significantly centred. The secondary green may be a product of mixing the blue and yellow pigments.

The work beckons freedom and suggests a sense of relief in style and mood. Although small and simple it conveys expansive ebullience and a release of the stasis intimated in the more sombre *Still Life with Steer's Skull* (1942).

STANDING WOMAN (1945)

Courtesy of Christie's Images

CONCEIVED in 1945 and cast in a numbered edition of ten, the bronze is a continuation of work that Picasso started during the war. His close friend and secretary, Jaime Sabartés, encouraged him to cast his developing sculpture work in bronze to protect it all after the Germans seized Picasso's Boisgeloup chateau, north-west of Paris and smashed several plaster pieces. However, as the Nazis had decreed all statues were to be melted down to recover metal for military purposes, Picasso's friends had to secrete the original plasters to a foundry in hand carts at the dead of night.

Probably as an act of defiance, Picasso produced bronze and copper work, as well as other sculpture media, during the war, continuing well into the 1950s until his interest in ceramics took over.

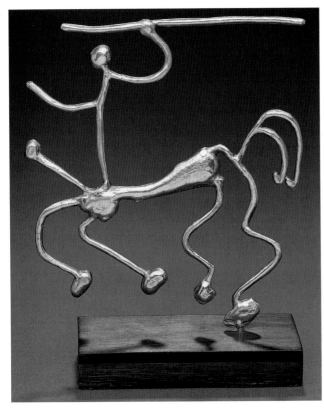

This particular work is a good example of his toy-like sculptural style. The piece has a rough and ready primitivism and is about 17.5 cm (7 in) high, with a dark brown patina. The button-like form of the face is repeated in the breast shape, and the figure, though cast in metal, maintains the plasticity and pliability of the modelling clay, giving it a notion of animation, an expression incorporated into other models like the gold *Centaure* (1961–67).

Centaure (1961–1967)
Courtesy of Christie's Images. (See p. 230)

JOIE DE VIVRE (1946)

Picasso Museum, Antibes. Courtesy of Giraudon

THIS work, obviously a parody of Matisse's celebrated work *Bonheur de Vivre* (1905–06), is often read as a celebration of peace. Matisse's lyrical work features nubile girls dancing and playing pipes in an idyllic setting as long, sensual curvaceous lines flow through the composition. Picasso's copy is more overtly mythological, featuring with pipe-playing fauns and dancing creatures. However, he captures Matisse's lyricism in the extended swirling lines of the figures, whose forms appear to grow organically like flowers moving upwards towards the Mediterranean sun.

Picasso had finally returned to his favoured French Riviera to enjoy freedom from Occupation as well as a burgeoning relationship with a young French artist, Françoise Gilot, whom he painted as a flower in 1946. She is possibly the model for the central creature of this work, with its long flowing hair. The couple visited Matisse in Nice – it was probably Matisse's request to paint Françoise with green hair that provoked Picasso to copy his rival's earlier work with this large 120 x 250 cm (4 x 9 ft) oil on fibreboard.

Picasso, 65 years old, an age when most retire, was once more in love with a very young woman and full of creative fervour. Françoise, 25, found she was pregnant shortly after this work was finished.

DETAIL OF WOMAN WITH A MANTILLA (1949)

Private Collection. Courtesy of Giraudon

*T*HIS picture represents Picasso's growing love of ceramics, a supple medium that allowed him to explore his playful notions of plasticity of form. His interest was kindled in 1947 while on the French Riviera near the pottery village of Vallauris. Here, he collaborated with the Madoura studio of Georges and Suzanne Ramié, whose chief potter helped Picasso to realise his designs. During the next few years he produced thousands of ceramic objects, painting on pots, plates, bowls and tiles.

Picasso was fascinated with Vallauris's ancient connections – it had been a major Roman centre for the production and exportation of amphora jars, made from the fine local pink clay. He explored Classical forms and styles in his work, as mythological images became stable sources for interpretation. This 47-cm (19-in) figure, a Hellenistic style 'tanagras' terracotta figurine, recalls the colouring of these ancient works as well as Picasso's earlier women; the eyes are reminiscent of *Portrait of Dora Maar* (1941).

Picasso established his own studio in Vallauris with Françoise Gilot, their son Claude and daughter

Portrait of Dora Maar (1941)
Courtesy of Christie's Images. (See p. 179)

Paloma, in order to develop his new love of ceramics, inventing oxides, glazes and enamels. The artist never actually threw his own pots, but had the pieces sent to him from nearby Madoura after creation, and then dispatched them back for firing.

THE SHE-GOAT (1950)

Picasso Museum, Paris. Courtesy of Giraudon

*P*ICASSO'S deepening interest in Classical imagery continued to make its presence felt in his sculpture as well as in his ceramic work. This massive life-size bronze is a wonderful assemblage of a wicker basket body, a palm leaf back, two ceramic flowerpots for the udder, and other metal elements, which was then cast. Apparently most of the objects were found in fields near Picasso's Vallauris studio.

The goat motif, like the bull, has been deeply embedded in European art since Classical times. Here, Picasso's goat is pregnant and is definitely a representation of his new, rising surge of optimism and love of life, following the war and his relationship with his young mistress, Françoise Gilot. Françoise had just had their second child, Paloma (the Spanish word for 'dove'), named after the Picasso poster, *Dove of Peace*, which appeared all around Paris in 1949 for the post-war Peace Congress. Thus, ancient themes of ritual, fertility and renewal of life, as in the featured series of plates (also decorated during this period) were regularly explored. The goat image is repeated later in the simple, gold form of *Centaure* (1961–1967).

Other 1950 assemblages also exuded a wonderful youthful energy and included *Woman with a Pushchair*, sentimentally created out of cake pans and a stove plate and cast in bronze.

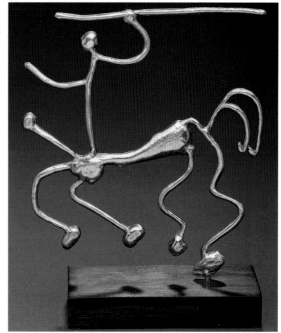

Centaure (1961–1967)
Courtesy of Christie's Images. (See p. 230)

THE BALUSTRADE (1953)

Courtesy of Christie's Images

*T*HIS brilliantly coloured, yet simplistic work is like other Picasso landscapes in that it seems to mark time between one style and another. Probably painted at Vallauris, it has a splendid energy, capturing the vibrant intensity of a Mediterranean summer whose light can be magical in its ability to enhance colour.

The deep azure of the sky resonates against the monochromatic green, the same hue used for the landscape and the lone tree, which rises like a bizarre-shaped parasol over the green below. The buildings are rose pink in the light. However, the force of the blue seems to subsume these colours, drawing in their energy. The lack of detail also sharpens this intensity of colour. Even the occasional black or green brush stroke here and there, defining the hillside opposite or points of foliage, does not detract from its vigour.

This is another work that seems to be indebted to Matisse, recalling some of the latter's early colour explorations, such as *The Dance* (1909), whose vibrancy makes the dancers almost fly off the canvas. Matisse was at this time bedridden in Nice and Picasso often visited him. He died in November 1954.

BULLFIGHT ARENA AND DOVE ON A BED OF HAY
(1950)
Courtesy of Christie's Images

*D*URING the 1950s Picasso played with plate decoration, exploring old and new motifs, particularly those with a Classical or mythological flavour as in the *Bullfight Arena* ceramic. Here, we see a mythological centaur, half man and half horse, killing the bull instead of Picasso's usual imagery from a modern day corrida. It is an unusual clash of Classical and nationalistic imagery.

This concept is repeated around the rim, where the simplistic peasant figures, mainly in Spanish costume, are set anachronistically to watch an ancient spectacle. Picasso enjoyed adapting the shape of the plate so that natural aspects of its design and form could become illusionistic settings for the rest of the composition, as here with the audience seated round the plate edge.

The shape of the *Dove on a Bed of Hay* plate has been adapted to denote the bird's nest. The bird had already become a major symbol for international concord after Picasso's poster, *Dove of Peace*, was pasted around Paris to herald the 1949 Peace Congress. As an extension of the pigeon imagery, the bird is also a motif for childhood – because of Picasso's father's obsession while Picasso was a child and because of Paloma's birth.

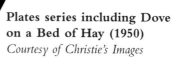

Plates series including Dove on a Bed of Hay (1950)
Courtesy of Christie's Images

TORMENTED FAUN AND ARRASTRE
(1956 and 1959)
Courtesy of Christie's Images

*O*NCE again, Picasso uses the plate to explore the sculptural aspects of its medium, so that the painting takes on a three-dimensional effect. *Arrastre* is another Picasso study of the bullfight, with the contours of the plate dynamically creating the moment of 'arrastre', when the dead animal is dragged off at the end of the fight. The dead bull falls off the plate rim into the pit of the arena, highlighted further by the streaked line of the bright yellow glaze. The raised, relief dotting of the horse and surrounding figures enhances their sculptural aspects, and, interestingly, presages the globular nature of the later metal work, *Centaure* (1961–67).

This work is probably part of a bullfight series Picasso created to commemorate his return to the village of Céret in the Pyrenées in 1953, which he had visited during the Cubist summers of 1911–13. By now a famous communist, he was invited back as guest of honour by the local communist party.

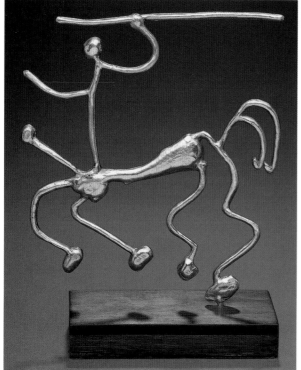

Picasso used the ceramic medium to practise images and techniques for future work. For instance, the *Face of a Tormented Faun* plate, with its relief beading, striations and patterning, was later converted to the flat linear work of *Man Wearing a Hat* (1956).

Centaure (1961–67)
Courtesy of Christie's Images.
(See p. 230)

WOMAN AND MONKEY (1954)
Courtesy of Christie's Images

*T*HIS is part of the *Verve Painter and Model* series of drawings, which, from November 1953 until February 1954, represented a full-blooded return to Picasso's traditional themes of circus, harlequins and mythology. Carried out in pen and ink, this work explores, like the others, the confrontation or gulf between the painter and his model; the distance between reality and the final illusion captured on the canvas. At this time, Françoise Gilot had just left him, old and alone with his fame. It was a dark juncture.

For most of his life Picasso had been romantically involved with his models, often taking younger women and moulding them to his needs, in the same way that as an artist he recreated the real models as art. The metaphor fascinated him and its irony is ingrained in this series to humorous effect, alongside other comically observed aesthetic issues. For instance, the monkey depicted here sometimes plays the artist in response to critical attacks concerning Picasso's style. The artist is also humorously depicted, sometimes old and decrepit, sometimes wild and savage, as here, with his hairy face peering over the canvas line at the top left. The image is reminiscent of the Minotaur and revisited in later works such as the *Lion's Head* ceramic tile (1956).

Lion's Head Ceramic (1968)
Courtesy of Christie's Images. (See p. 212)

SYLVETTE (1954)

Courtesy of Christie's Images

*T*HIS is one of a series of 40 drawings and oils of Sylvette David, a 21-year-old girl who posed for Picasso during April 1954. This odd work acknowledges his Cubist roots but also recalls the lyrical 1930s images of Marie-Thérèse and Dora Maar, as in *The Muse* (1935). He had no emotional relationship with Sylvette but became fascinated with her profile and ponytail, examining her form using various artistic techniques, from realism to intense geometrical studies.

In this particular piece, Picasso works on splitting Sylvette's profile into three-dimensional relief, as if the whole image has been fractured into front, back and sides and then laid out flat on the canvas surface. Next to the face we see the ear and then the black construction lines which grid out to form the pony tail and hair falling down the back. In *The Muse* we see a similar fracturing of the body to open up different aspects of the figure's perspective.

This sculptural quality is later realised in true three-dimensional format with the construction of this portrait as a huge outdoor concrete bust for New York University, USA. The work was constructed in 1968 by the young Norwegian artist Carl Nesjar, who perfected sandblasting techniques to reproduce art on concrete.

The Muse (1935) *Gallery of Modern Art, Paris. Courtesy of Topham. (See p. 140)*

PROFILE OF JACQUELINE (1956)
Courtesy of Christie's Images

JACQUELINE Roque, a young divorcée, first entered Picasso's life in 1953. As his relationship with Françoise Gilot deteriorated, she eventually returned to Paris with the children and he found Jacqueline increasingly attractive. By 1954, they were living together in Paris and she inevitably became his next and final muse. Olga finally died in 1955, leaving Picasso available, but he did not marry Jacqueline until 1961, five years later and just before his 80th birthday.

This ceramic plaque highlights Jacqueline's stunning southern Mediterranean beauty, which was frequently transformed by Picasso over the ensuing years into sphinx-like images featuring her heavy oriental-type eyes and graceful neck. Her strong Classical profile haunted Picasso and he was convinced that she had figured in his mind for many years prior to their meeting, often showing her his earlier work to demonstrate similarities.

The partial glazing of this ceramic, executed in Vallauris, is a fascinating use of colour, relating back to the 1930s images of Marie-Thérèse, such as *Sleeping Before Green Shutters* (1936), with its watery merging of the thin blues and greens. As in *Sleeping Before Green Shutters*, the effect creates a heavy melancholic sense of sadness, again reminiscent of Picasso's very early Blue Period.

Sleeping before Green Shutters
(Marie-Thérèse Walter) (1936)
Picasso Museum, Paris. Courtesy of Giraudon. (See p. 142)

19.2.56.II

LION'S HEAD CERAMIC (1968)

Courtesy of Christie's Images

BEGINNING in 1956, Picasso progressed from his ceramic studies to earthenware floor tiles, known as *tomettes*, as a new art form. He was interested in the planar and sculptural qualities that the tiles offered, carving, gouging and painting them. The employment of his range of Classical and mythological motifs suited the Romanesque, crude, low-fired, red brick tiles, and they were transformed into owls, heads, Bacchanals and bullfighting scenes. Picasso played with the tile's shape and design to create illusions, in this case turning a square tile on its end and filling the space with the round form of the lion's head. The work played ingeniously on form and geometric concepts of squaring the circle.

Picasso would often carve the comparatively soft material of the unfired tile, as probably in this case, with simple, reductionist, yet highly effective designs. The deep striations conjure up the burly animalistic power of the king of the jungle, which, like the Minotaur imagery, is half man and signifies Picasso's life-long contemplation of man's nature and ego. The facial characteristics are also seen in productions like *Man with Hat* (1956), again underscoring the figure's bestial attributes.

Man with Hat (1956)
Courtesy of Christie's Images. (See p. 219)

THE DANCE (1956)

Courtesy of Christie's Images

THE lyricism of this drawing recalls Picasso's main tribute to Matisse, *Joie de Vivre* (1946), which was executed at the end of the Second World War as a celebration of peace. Like the former work, the swirling lines are stretched and extended into a pliable form, though here, they are probably Picasso's final farewell to Matisse, who died in 1954. He was deeply touched by the loss of this old friend and rival, and increasingly felt isolated from the old guard as many of his contemporaries died.

Matisse himself completed a series of works entitled *Dance* during his career, a theme which he regularly developed in order to study colour techniques through accentuated contours. A massive Matisse mural for an American commission in the early 1930s has a very similar animated figuration to this Picasso work. In it Matisse used cut-out shapes to study the movement of the dancing figures within the available space, similarly invoked by these Picasso figures.

However, whereas Matisse incessantly studied mobility in colour, the cut-out figures shown here, are another example of Picasso's life-long obsession with form. Their simple, flowing lines conjure up a beautiful, melodic rhythm of musical animation.

Joie de Vivre (1946)
Picasso Museum, Antibes. Courtesy of Giraudon. (See p. 194)

SUNSET (1956)

Courtesy of Christie's Images

THE tremendous energy of this landscape is undoubtedly influenced by Vincent Van Gogh, who made such an impact on the early development of Picasso. He revered Van Gogh and was in awe of the unassuming nature of his iconoclastic art and lifestyle. Picasso often joked that if the impoverished artist had lived to enjoy his own level of success, he would still never have driven around in a Rolls Royce. In 1955 Picasso and Jacqueline had moved to La Californie, the spectacular nineteenth-century villa in Cannes with views of Golfe-Juan and Antibes. A room overlooking the large garden with eucalyptus and palm trees was converted into the next studio; *Sunset* was one of many paintings he produced here.

The setting for this landscape is no doubt in the Cannes locality and, as critics point out, underlines Picasso's main interest in a scene's physiognomic attributes rather than its typical qualities. Here, Picasso sections the landscape into horizontal colour blocks with the central, heavily blackened form of the church acting as the main opposite vertical movement. The whole picture is a careful balance of eddying polarised colours and strong geometric forms, as vertical and horizontal tensions grid the surface.

MAN WITH A HAT (1956)

Courtesy of Christie's Images

THIS wildly vital piece deliberately recreates simplistic elements of a child's drawing through the use of coloured crayons on paper and laid down on canvas. With the basketwork features, feathering of the lines and the minimalist use of the two colours red and blue, the work invokes earlier, more complex prototypes of the technique, such as the portrait of Dora Maar, *Seated Woman* (1938).

Here, the bestial-like face completely fills the surface of the paper as the child-like doodles web and weave to create it. Again, Picasso plays subtly with geometric notions of squaring the circle: although the large head is round, a thin blue line marks squares the facial region before it is filled in with noughts, crosses, curls, heart shapes and feathering.

The roguish hairy face is one of Picasso's favourite motifs, particularly when exploring notions of beauty and the beast, or artist and model. It is a self-projection technique, almost like an alter ego, which surfaced in many drawings over the years and recurs increasingly in his last works. Sometimes the bestial or animal side is more prominent, as in the *Lions Head* ceramic (1956), or the human qualities are uppermost, as in the manic work *Man's Head* (1969).

Seated Woman (1938)
Norman Granz Private Collection. Courtesy of Topham. (See p. 164)

LA TAUROMAQUIA (1957–60)

Picasso Museum, Barcelona. Courtesy of AiSA

THIS work is taken from a bullfighting collection produced for a Spanish publication called *La Tauromaquia* (The Art of Bullfighting) which came out in late 1959, with a sequel in 1961.

Picasso worked on the project regularly during this period, beautifully recreating animated scenes from his lifelong passion of bullfighting. The publication also enabled him to re-examine a variety of engraving print methods, including etching, dry-point and aquatints, as well as pen and ink. Dry-point etching is the use of a steel stylus on unpolished copper plate so that ink is caught in the scratched copper 'burrs' to create a characteristic bloom to the line. Aquatint uses acid in the etching combined with stopping techniques so that darkening degrees of tone can be achieved.

The process allowed Picasso to concentrate on capturing a moment, as with his ceramic work *Arrastre* (c. 1953), but with more realistic detail. The techniques involved great focus and precision and the results are stunning. The black and white format reproduces delicate images instead of the brutality of the bullfight, and captures its supposed hypnotic appeal. This particular work, which is not in Zervos, Picasso's cataloguer, is possibly pen and wash, another technique that emphasises sensations of grace and finesse.

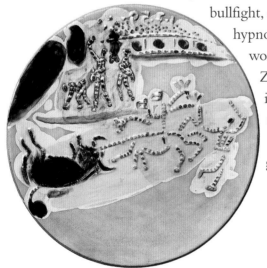

Arrastre Ceramic Plate (1959)
Courtesy of Christie's Images. (See p. 204)

NUDE WITH UPLIFTED ARMS (1959)

Private Collection. Courtesy of Giraudon

TOWARDS the end of his career, Picasso enjoyed examining Classical works that had influenced his development over the years, playing at being Goya, El Greco or Manet, the founder of modern traditions. However, this work clearly recalls *Les Demoiselles d'Avignon* (1907), the profile of the face and rudiments of this nude resembling the central nude from his celebrated early masterpiece. It is as though Picasso was actually playing at being Picasso, the old master, as he revisited his own classics.

His conversations of the time certainly underscored his realisation that he had arrived and would be measured alongside the company of old Renaissance masters whom he had respected and learned from. Probably the greatest artist of the twentieth century, Picasso's place in art history was assured. Within his own lifetime he recognised both this and the influence he had on the aesthetic developments of the younger generations, yet he continued to set his own iconoclastic pace.

Here, this nude's frontal features are very explicit, as in many of his early erotic drawings, with the exposed armpits, pudenda and rear. These have been configured here into a three-dimensional perspective, as in the *Sylvette* works (1954), so that all views of the bottom section of the body are seen.

Les Demoiselles d'Avignon (1907)
The Museum of Modern Art, New York. Acquired through the Lillie P. Bliss Bequest. Courtesy of the Museum of Modern Art, New York. (See p. 60)

GUITAR PLAYER AND PEOPLE
IN A LANDSCAPE (1960)
Courtesy of Christie's Images

*T*HIS dark, mad, free-flowing pastoral is illustrative of the heavier tonal style which Picasso progressed through to the end of his productive life. Although the subject matter appears unrefined and child-like, there is a saturnine feel in the way the colours from a darker palette soak the surface. This is emphasised by the use of heavy black rimming, either to create outlines, as in the figures here, or for hatching out areas of definition.

Later work sees Picasso's attempts to liberate himself from earlier experiments concerning form and colour, and shows a renewed interest in the Old Masters. His concerns with Manet surface in this piece, which was probably a follow-on from the period's pastiches of Manet's *Déjeuner sur l'Herbe*. The work also conjures up the painting style of Van Gogh, with its wavy, foaming swathes of colour and violent brushwork, especially the sky section which creates a sense of foreboding and oppression over the superficially happy pastoral scene. The bizarre, unsophisticated figures are either outlined in black and left with blank white spaces, or almost totally closed in with black, like the menacing guitar player standing behind the children as they play innocently on the ground. One feels his musical tones are as mysterious and dark as the colours the artist uses.

PROFILE OF A WOMAN'S FACE (1960)
Courtesy of Christie's Images

THE theme of the painter and his model again surfaces throughout these later works. The model here is, of course, the last great love of his life, Jacqueline Roque, whom he quietly married in 1961, the year after this picture was completed. Her strong southern Mediterranean features are sharply profiled in a series of sphinx-like portraits. This work, continuing Picasso's lively interest in the imagery of antiquity, is similar to classical Egyptian representations of Queen Cleopatra with her enlarged, heavily kohl-lined eye.

The flat, planar approach of this painting, constructed from a few simple lines, is emphasised by Picasso's return to a tri-colour scheme. Again, the polarising force of red and green accents the lack of depth, throwing the profile into stronger relief. This technique was borrowed from Matisse and used to great effect with the Marie-Thérèse portraits of the 1930s, such as *Rest* (1932) in which the energy from the two horizontal bands of colour stressed the stillness of the model lying asleep between them. Similarly, here, the whiteness of Jacqueline's face is lifted from the sea of intense green by the redness of the hat, resulting in a specific stress on the profile – and hence the picture's title.

Asleep (1932)
Courtesy of Christie's Images (see p. 128)

THE PIGEONS (1960)
Courtesy of Christie's Images

T HIS landscape was painted at the fourteenth-century chateau of Vauvenargues, which lies in the shadow of Cézanne's Mont Sainte-Victoire close to Aix-en-Provence in the south of France. Picasso purchased this fabulous house in 1958 and filled the sumptuous rooms with paintings and sculptures brought from Paris. These were idyllic times of prosperity and fame for Picasso, with retrospectives of his work regularly hosted around the world. He was to be buried at Vauvenargues in 1973.

Interestingly, nearly all Picasso's landscapes were executed in the south of France. A combination of the light, warmth and a relaxed lifestyle conjures up impressions of sweet happiness and tranquillity, which exude from works such as this. There is a sense of stillness and serenity as the passive, blank, white forms of the pigeons create gentle hollows in the dark swirling colours of the setting. Again, elements of the style of Van Gogh, who was himself deeply affected by the region's intensity of light, seep into this work, recalling the latter's *Starry Night:* a deep cobalt blue, night-time sky, overlaid with yellow flicks of the brush to signify the stars. Although similar in colour and setting to *The Balustrade* (1953), the deeper hues and secondary framing of the composition, created by the insertion of the veranda's ochre surround, conveys a deeper, more complex perspective.

The Balustrade (1953)
Courtesy of Christie's Images. (See p. 200)

CENTAURE (1961–1967)

Courtesy of Christie's Images

FIVE-and-a-half inches (14.2 cm) in height this beautiful but simple model of a centaur has been cast in 18-carat gold. It is one of a limited edition of ten, executed over a six-year period, and bears the goldsmith's mark of François and Pierre Hugo. It is not known if these precious objects were private gifts, but it is interesting that the move into gold came in Picasso's 80th year, a celebrated event, and the year of his marriage to Jacqueline.

The ancient Greek Homeric figure sees a return to Picasso's pictorial quest into mythology, a feature from many of his 1950s studies in ceramics. This medium allowed him to explore three-dimensional aspects of painting, as in the illustrated plate, *Bullfight Arena*. This wonderful golden statue ironically reverses the process as the traditional three-dimensional aspect of modelling is reduced to two-dimensional linear relief by employing the thin piped effect of the gold. However, despite the simplicity of line, Picasso captures the dynamic action of this half-horse, half-man brilliantly. The inclusion of its phallic extra 'leg', a favourite ancient Greek fertility device, continues the artist's 'man as beast' theme as well as emphasising the centaurs' drunken brawl at a wedding.

Ceramic Plates (1950)
414 Bullfight Arena
Courtesy of Christie's Images. (See p. 202)

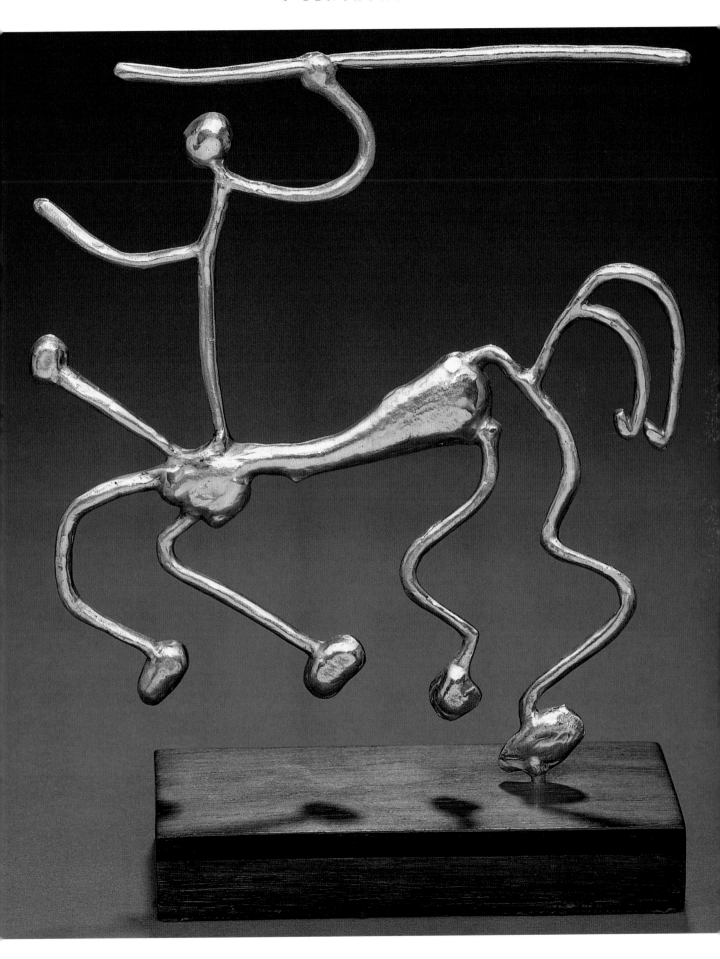

SELECTION OF CERAMIC TILES (1960s)

Courtesy of Christie's Images

272 MASQUE RIEUR
273 VISAGE AUX TRAITS EN X

*P*ICASSO turned his attention to painting on small ceramic plaques as he pursued his interest in ceramics at the end of his life. He had several series in production, again exploring and developing many of the themes from his current repertoire of oil paintings. He enjoyed playing with the medium to study both planar and sculptural issues and how they interrelated.

Because of their rectangular format, the tiles initially appear to be two-dimensional paintings. However, they are slabs of brick with a rectangular section carved out of the centre, which is then removed. The remaining grainy irregularities are incorporated as artistic features, instead of being smoothed away, before re-firing.

Here, Picasso started to play with the musketeer and bearded

man imagery that recurs regularly throughout the 1960s until his death. For instance, features like the simplistic combined eyebrow and nose line from the *Masque Rieur* (*Laughing Mask*), appear in later works, such as *Man's Head* (c. 1965), where its simple shape creates a more sinister effect. The adaptation of the tile's square form to denote a circular face shape is an extension of the artist's earlier playful but artistic endeavours to make the circle square, as in the comic drawing, *Man with a Hat* (1956).

Man's Head (c. 1965)
Courtesy of Christie's Images (see p. 244)

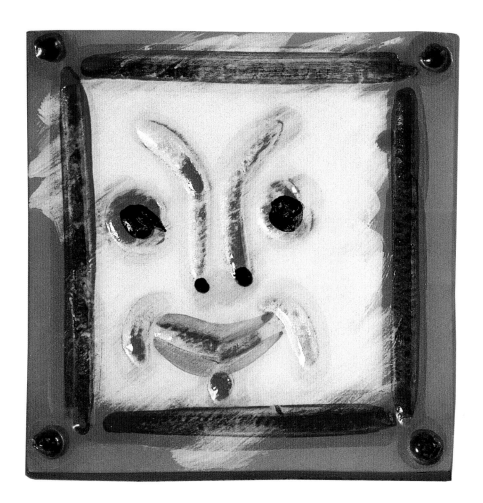

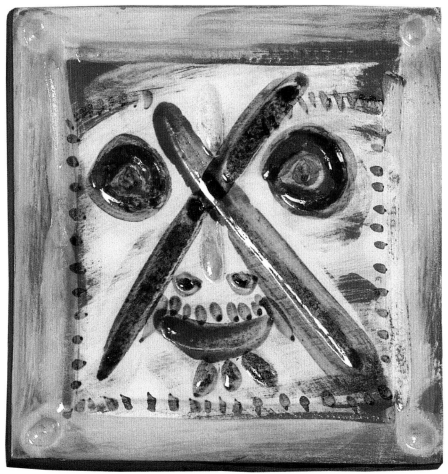

233

SELECTION OF CERAMIC TILES (1960s)

Courtesy of Christie's Images

HORSE AND RIDER
LITTLE SUN FACE
LITTLE SUN FACE

*A*S IN the previous tiles, Picasso enjoyed playing with the ceramic medium to study how planar and sculptural issues interrelate. Here, we see the repetition of many themes from this period of Picasso's work. The sun faces joyfully recall images from other ceramic works, like the *Lion's Head* ceramic (1956), as well as *Man with a Hat* (1956), the fun *Head of a Bearded Man* (1964) and the more bestial images, such as *Man's Head* (c. 1965). The effect is one of radiance, evocative of long Mediterranean summers.

The horse and rider is an interesting experiment in form and could have been a pre-cursor to the more dynamic series of gold statues, *Centaure* (1961–1967). Here, the golden colour is captured using a bright glaze, and the raised legs, neck profile and distinctive globular hooves have strong parallels with the later piped gold model. The image could also relate to Picasso's increasing interest in literature from the Spanish Golden Age, which drew on musketeer motifs.

During this time, Picasso worked on his ceramics in two studios; first at La Californie until 1961 and then at his final home, Notre-Dame-de-Vie in Mougins on the French Riviera, which he bought in 1961 and where he was to die in 1973.

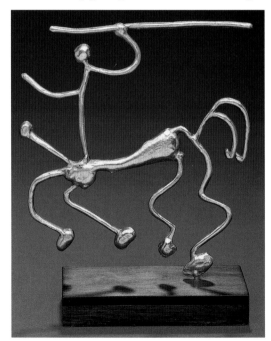

CENTAURE (1961–1967)
Courtesy of Christie's Images. (See p. 230)

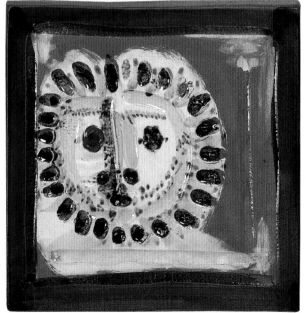

HEAD OF A SEATED WOMAN (1962)

Courtesy of Christie's Images

*T*HIS work forms part of a series of 70 portraits of Jacqueline carried out in 1962. The reduction and distortion of the facial characteristics and the simplicity of colour are reminiscent of the late 1930s series of portraits of Dora Maar and Marie-Thérèse, and the hair recalls the ponytail from the paintings of Sylvette in 1954. The focus on the eye as a singled-out feature is a device repeated from *Profile of a Woman's Face* (1960).

In a similar way, colour has been employed to enhance the 'seeing' eye effect, with the strong green background resonating against the yellowy-reds of the hat and then accentuated on the face below the eye. The heavy black delineation conjoining the eye with the neck exaggerates the effect further, making the eye stand out as though on a stalk, or appear as if it is a work of sculpture attached to a pyramidal-shaped plinth.

The face is close to the surface of the picture and, with the oddly shaped hat and cut-away whiteness of the stalked neck, the figure resembles images of a queen from a deck of playing cards or a sculptured chess piece. The folding of the facial features and head is also dynamically explored in a series of sheet-metal sculptures of the same time.

Profile of a Woman's Face (1960)
Courtesy of Christie's Images. (See p. 226)

HEAD (1962–64)

Illinois, U.S.A.. Courtesy of Topham

PICASSO'S later work, using sheet metal, and his life-long development in 'landscape' studies of the face are suitably realised in his first commissioned piece of civic sculpture, for Chicago, Illinois, USA. This massive work, constructed outside the city's civic centre in the new business district, was also inspired by his continuing collaboration with Norwegian designer, Carl Nesjar, who transformed Picasso's *Sylvette* (1954) into a concrete statue for New York University and was also involved in converting other works into international construction pieces.

Picasso worked on a maquette, or model, for the *Head* sculpture between 1962 and 1964, fashioned after a 1962 metal cut-out, *Head of a Woman*. The final version, in welded steel and standing 20 m (60 ft) high, was completed in 1965 and unveiled in 1967.

The work draws on many of Picasso's artistic experiments over the years, with its dislocation and distortion of form, the basketwork structure connecting the minimalist facial contours with the huge steel wing-like structures for the hair, as seen in the *Sylvette* pictures. Its bestial, praying-mantis features also recall Picasso's Surrealist ventures of the late 1920s. It is a fitting summation of so much that has come to signify Picasso's art.

Sylvette (1954)
Courtesy of Christie's Images. (See p. 209)

HEAD OF A BEARDED MAN (1964)

Courtesy of Christie's Images

*T*HIS amusing face, executed in pastels on paper, is reminiscent of *Man with a Hat* (1956), whose simplicity was expressed with crayon. This later work is a deliberate attempt to recreate a child's drawing, with its roughly formed lines scratched under the beard on the chest and the multi-coloured scribbles for hair and eyebrows. The zigzagging central blue and purple lines depict a dual profile of the nose, with the pastels' crude coloured-in strokes clearly visible.

This cartoon-like portrait is probably another of Picasso's self-projections, particularly with the balding head and wispy sides, which correspond to photographic images of Picasso at the time. These works became simple dramatic masks for the artist to present his recurrent theme of bestial man. However, the child-like elements also reveal the real Picasso – a youthful, energetic spirit, seeking constant creative fulfilment while stuck behind the mask of old age.

At this point Picasso was 83, but he seemed at least 20 years younger. He still exuded so much vitality, thanks, as before, to the influence of a younger woman, who provided him with much creative inspiration, as well as sexual confidence, to stave off his greatest fear: death.

Man with a Hat (1956)
Courtesy of Christie's Images. (See p. 219)

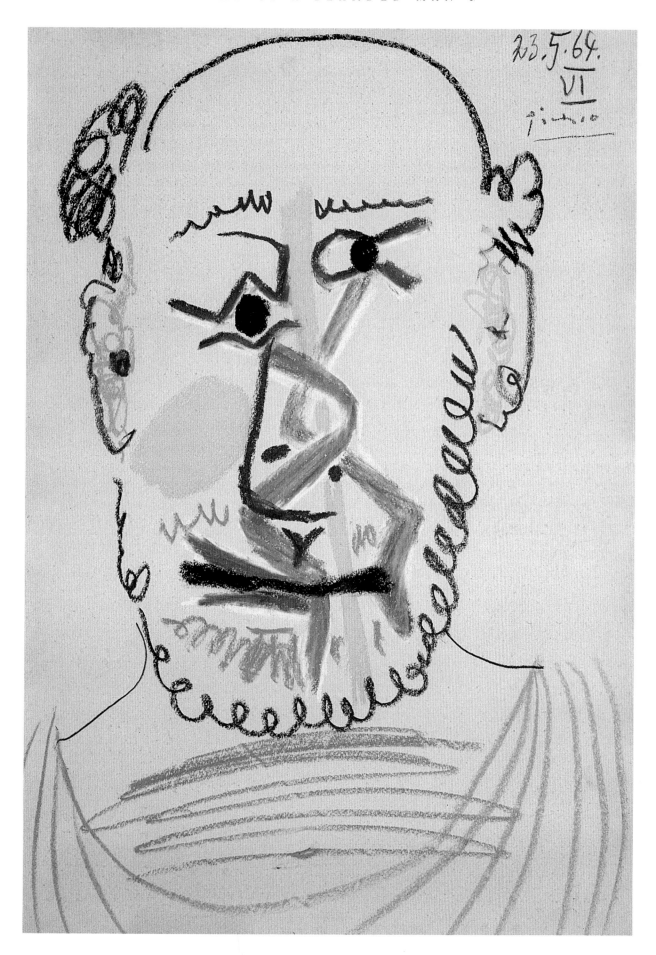

WOMAN'S BUST (1965)

Courtesy of Christie's Images

THIS is one of 30 canvasses on the theme of the 'artist and his model', painted within a month. The face is Jacqueline's, but also recalls many earlier images from his oeuvre, such as *Les Demoiselles d'Avignon* (1907). The new, looser form of his work is apparent and there is a return of earlier plasticity, as the lines remain fluid and shapes are often defined linearly but left devoid of colour.

As in other pictures of the 1960s, Picasso uses a progressively darker palette, although here a greater variety of pigments are used to make the picture feel tonally brighter than other oils of the time. Probably the most striking feature is, once again, the intensity of the face, with its odd, deep turquoise colour and the large, heavy-rimmed black eyes. The use of deep carmine red to frame areas around the face, such as the headscarf and aspects of the room, further enhances this effect. Somehow this colour combination creates a cavernous feel, making the profile recede and giving an impression of depth and mystery. Picasso returns to a similar colour formation in one of his last *Painter and his Model* works in 1969, where the nude is truly distanced from the surface of the canvas and from the viewer.

Painter and his Model (1968)
Courtesy of Christie's Images. (See p. 249)

MAN'S HEAD (C. 1965)

Courtesy of Christie's Images

THIS is another of Picasso's child-like paintings of a man's face, in which the form is reduced to a few linear strokes, dots and swirls to indicate expression and character. The use of oil, particularly the flatter colours from his new darker palette, instead of pastel or crayon, gives this face a more serious countenance compared to the cartoon-like figure in *Head of a Bearded Man* (1964), which conveyed fun and youthful, buoyant energy.

Despite complete simplicity of form and style, this work seems more raw than the childish scribbles of *Head of a Bearded Man*. The paint has been daubed roughly on the canvas, the brush marks are clearly obvious, as is the texture of the unpainted canvas in many areas. Similarly, the man's expression is coarse and rugged. There is also a dark vitality, strength and sexual tension about the expression, particularly caught by the heavy black handling of key facial characteristics, such as the strong eyebrows, nose line, mouth and eye, and the dark smudges representing hair and beard.

During 1965, Picasso, aged 84, was not in good health; he was admitted to a Paris hospital for an ulcer operation in November. It was to be his last time in Paris.

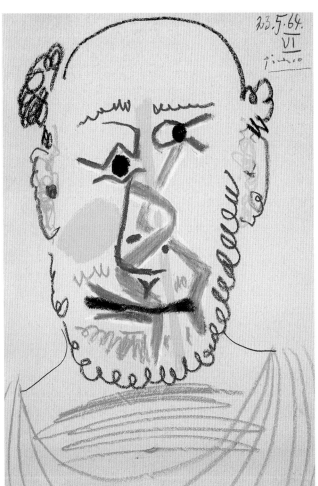

Head of a Bearded Man (1964)
Courtesy of Christie's Images. (See p. 240)

LANDSCAPE (1967)

Courtesy of Christie's Images

*T*OWARDS the end of his life, Picasso spent most of his time at his villa, Notre-Dame-de-Vie, in Mougins on the French Riviera, which was bought in 1961 after La Californie suffered from over-development around Cannes. It was at Notre-Dame-de-Vie that Picasso died in 1973. The place, due to the surrounding views, was the inspiration for many later works, particularly this fabulous landscape.

Picasso was not known as a landscape artist, being more interested in the pastoral epic such as *Guernica* (1937) or parodying styles by Van Gogh or Manet. The landscape of the body became his true life's work. However, in this picture, there is a wonderful sense that Picasso finally breaks free from some self-imposed constraint or theory about landscape and discovers a real voice of his own. There is a harmony and stillness as if the scene is melting before his eyes into myriad forms and colours, while it fades into the universal. Just before his death, Picasso seems to have recognised something fundamental and spiritual that transcends time. The white mass, possibly of the Mougins villa, almost fades into this timeless, sylvan scene, signifying the imperviousness of nature to human constructions. This spiritual quality is conjured up by the cool hues, particularly the use of turquoise to create depth.

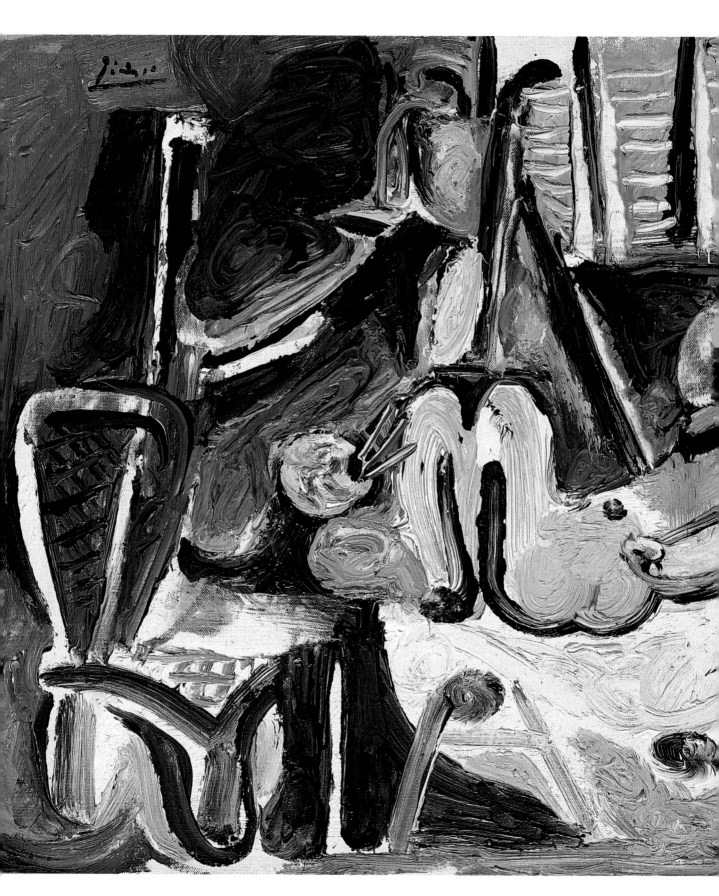

PAINTER AND HIS MODEL (1968)
Courtesy of Christie's Images

WHEN considering the length of Picasso's life and the series of beautiful woman he used as models, it is no wonder that the mystery of the relationship between artist and model continually fascinated him. It was the main thrust of his work, spilling out in oils, drawings, etchings and sculpture, from his early days in Spain and Paris through to this, one of his final explorations.

In his later freer style, as form and colour connect and flow loosely across the canvas, Picasso viewed this scene with more depth and volume than in many of his earlier works. By introducing this distance, he finally seems to become less passionate and more objective about the subject.

Here, the model is hardly visible with her slack outline, filled with the cool turquoise Picasso now enjoyed using to create mystery and depth. It is as if her form is hardly relevant as she physically manifests from the canvas onto the floor and then blends in with the backdrop of the studio. It is though Picasso has finally realised that her spirit needs to be set free rather than captured in the medium. His own insignificant black shape also merges into the surroundings.

Man's Head (1969)
Courtesy of Christie's Images. (See p. 252)

HEAD OF A MUSKETEER (1969)
Courtesy of Christie's Images

*T*HIS simple drawing has been created with green felt-tip pen on paper and is part of a series Picasso executed in his later years. The imagery possibly came from stories of the Golden Age of Spanish Literature or from the French classic *The Three Musketeers*, borrowed in the same way that he adapted Spanish traditions through bullfighting and the symbol of the mythological Minotaur.

The face of the musketeer appeared regularly in Picasso's drawings, paintings and on his ceramics. A large, tiled mural featuring a Cubist-like image of a musketeer was finished in the same year, 1969.

Like the Minotaur, the literary image becomes a mask worn by the painter to explore aesthetic and social issues concerning sexuality, tradition and manhood. Here, the lines are very simple to create this gentle smiling countenance, reminiscent of *Head of a Bearded Man* (1964). However in *Man's Head* (1969), drawn just two days after the musketeer's head, Picasso uses a felt-tip pen to conjure up something far more elaborate and primeval, as though the historical image of a musketeer has suddenly shot beyond time to become the image of the eternal Green Man, or Green Wolf, as he was known in France, a Bacchanalian character who grew organically from nature.

MAN'S HEAD (1969)

Courtesy of Christie's Images

*I*N THE same way that the wild, vital *Man with a Hat* (1956) filled the surface of the paper totally with its child-like doodles that web and weave, this fabulous, energetic *Man's Head* tendrils out into a complex, orgiastic drawing.

Working with felt-tip pen, instead of crayon as in the earlier piece, Picasso extends his fascination with basketwork configurations, feathering, and the minimalist use of colours to evolve this bestial character whose abundant organic form grows expansively out of its designated blue facial framework. It is a bizarre study in male fecundity and like the previous *Head of a Musketeer*, painted just two days earlier

on 15 June 1969, is an artistic mask for Picasso to explore notions of beauty and the beast. Here the face stands alone, but variations appear during this time, found in a series of highly explicit and erotic drawings concerning artist and model and the act of sexual intercourse.

Man's Head explores the theme of the primeval forces of nature, in the same way that Provençal locals celebrated the annual Midsummer coming of the eternal Green Man or Green Wolf, with bonfires and festivities.

Man with a Hat (1956)
Courtesy of Christie's Images. (See p. 219)

SEATED WOMAN WITH A HAT (1971)

Courtesy of Christie's Images

WITH this vibrant painting, Picasso shows that he has lost none of his extraordinary verve or creative energy. There is a fusion of his many earlier techniques in his final works, but still he constantly pushed at artistic boundaries to unearth new stylistic developments. He had come a long way from the portrait of his earlier mistress, Madeleine, *Woman in a Chemise* (1904–05).

Most of the later work continued with this strange palette, usually subdued and sombre but with sudden outbursts of colour, such as the yellow hat, red nails and mouth. Yet even these bright tones appear muted within the scheme of the composition.

Woman in a Chemise (1904-05)
Courtesy of the Tate Gallery, London. *(See p. 42)*

Memories of bygone days and lost loves surface in works like this. It harks back to the many portraits from the 1930s when Picasso was experimenting with rhythmic forms and strong primary colours while he shared his life with both Dora Maar and Marie-Thérèse Walter.

This large portrait, 129 cm x 96.8 cm (4 x 3 ft), was shown for the first time at an exhibition shortly after his death, aged 91, at Notre-Dame-de-Vie, on 8th April 1973 – an amazing and fitting tribute to the grand master of 20th-century art.

AUTHOR BIOGRAPHIES AND ACKNOWLEDGMENTS

'O misshapen chaos of well-seeming forms....'
(ROMEO & JULIET, WILLIAM SHAKESPEARE)

To my muse, family and Picasso lovers everywhere...

Laura Payne is a Picasso afficionade and UK-based writer, journalist and broadcaster, who has followed the arts movement for many years, travelling the world to view Picasso's work. She took time out from an international media career to pursue an MA in Literature and the Visual Arts, and now her current area of research is British and European early modernism, in which she is working on a new critical analysis and aesthetic theory.

Dr Julia Kelly was educated at Oxford and the Courtauld Institute of Art. She specialises in 20th-century art, in particular Surrealism and the inter-war period. Her PhD thesis was in the art writings of Michel Leiris. She has published works on Picasso and Francis Bacon.

While every endeavour has been made to ensure the accuracy of the reproduction of the images in this book, we would be grateful to receive any comments or suggestions for inclusion in future reprints.

With thanks to Image Select and Christie's Images for assistance with sourcing the pictures for this series of books. Grateful thanks also to Frances Banfield, Lucinda Hawksley and Sasha Heseltine.